PANORAMAS OF LOST LONDON

1870-1945

Historic England

PANORAMAS OF LOST LONDON

1870-1945

Philip Davies

ATLANTIC PUBLISHING

Acknowledgements

This publication is an abridged edition of *Lost London 1870-1945* first published in 2009.
All the photographs in this publication were taken from the collection of the former Greater
London Council Historic Buildings Division. Upon the abolition of the GLC in 1984 the
print collection was transferred to the London Region of English Heritage where it remains
in daily use for reference purposes. The negatives are held by the London Metropolitan
Archives. The illustrations in this book are protected by copyright and may only be
reproduced by permission of English Heritage or the London Metropolitan Archives.

Published by Atlantic Publishing 2018
Atlantic Publishing, 38 Copthorne Road, Croxley Green, Hertfordshire, WD3 4AQ

ISBN: 978-1-909242-75-3
Printed and bound in the Czech Republic

CONTENTS

INTRODUCTION

London, the first great metropolis of the industrial age, was never controlled by a single political or religious body able to guide the layout of its streets to one grand design. Instead, it was the largely-unplanned creation of a pluralist society driven by trade and commercial imperatives. In the aftermath of the Great Fire of 1666, the evanescent visions of Christopher Wren, Robert Hooke and John Evelyn evaporated like morning mist before the rising sun of commercial resurgence. London always was, and remains, a city founded on commerce, flourishing today as a world centre for the trading of financial services.

London's expansion in the 18th and 19th centuries was driven by speculative development. Pragmatic contracts between wealthy landowners and opportunistic builders were regulated by the leasehold system; the former in search of long-term income, and the latter by the prospect of turning a quick profit.

Narrow timber-framed houses were the established building type in London before the Great Fire. The average twelve-feet plot width was dictated by the maximum length of structural timber. A significant number of these houses survived the Fire well into the 20th century on the fringes of the City of London in Smithfield, Holborn, Aldgate and Borough, providing a very tangible link with the mediaeval past. Their distinctive gables and jettied upper storeys can be seen in the photographs, often heavily overlain by subsequent alterations. On the expiry of leases, it was quite common for such houses to be encased in brick, or given a polite facade, rather than completely redeveloped; many London houses, whilst ostensibly similar, embraced much older structures and interiors beneath – individual metaphors for the city as a whole.

In the wake of the Great Fire, various London Building Acts were passed – in 1667, 1707 and 1709 – specifying common standards of construction. Increasingly, brick replaced timber for external use which facilitated much greater external uniformity. The earliest surviving example of

Opposite: 195 Mile End Road, 12 November 1944. Demolished shortly after this photograph was taken, No. 195 was a rare surviving weatherboarded timber house of c.1700.

Right: Grove House, 36 Chatham Place, Hackney, c.1912. Grove House was one of the larger houses built on the St Thomas's Hospital estate in the early 18th century. In 1783 it became an academy for the deaf & dumb. After a brief period as a clothing factory, it passed to the Hackney Progressive Club, after which it fell vacant. It was demolished in 1921.

a row of matching London town houses can be found at Nos 52–55 Newington Green. Built in 1658, they pre-date the Fire, but in the reconstruction of London after 1666, the brick terrace became the established urban form, creating a key component of what made London unique as a European city.

Nicholas Barbon (d.1698), a financier, builder and adventurer, refined the system of speculative leasehold development through which much of Georgian and Victorian London was built. Various builders undertook to construct small numbers of houses within a particular development, often overseen by the landowner or his agent. In order to ensure consistency, the row of uniformly designed houses evolved and became fashionable. This form of housing was remarkably versatile, providing flexible accommodation for a whole variety of uses – houses, taverns, offices, shops and workshops – usually with a private rear yard, or garden. Short rows of terraced housing were built in central and inner London, but also as ribbon development in outlying areas along the main roads such as Mile End, Chiswick, Tottenham and Peckham.

Often minor variations in window heights or parapet levels marked the work of each builder, but the overall aspiration was greater uniformity. In the first half of the 18th century this trend towards understated regularity was

reinforced by the Palladian revival. Carved doorcases and other elaborate sculptural enrichment were eschewed in favour of external sobriety and abstract qualities of proportion.

In 1774 the Building Acts were consolidated into a new London Building Act which specified different "rates" of houses. This dictated the form and design of much of London for over a century and created the city which can be seen in these photographs. The floor area set the rate, which in turn determined the thickness of the principal walls. Like industrial products, a family of building types emerged – from the highest first-rate house with a five-bay frontage and a linked mews building to the modest fifth-rate dwelling just one room deep.

Much of Georgian and early Victorian London owes its remarkable unity to the increasingly standardised approach to elevations drawn up by estate surveyors. This is why 18th- and 19th-century housing looks so similar in areas as diverse as Camberwell, Bloomsbury and Bow. The serial construction of whole neighbourhoods of planned streets and squares on the private landed estates of central and inner London was a process of continuous refinement, and it created a distinctive city completely unlike anything else in Europe. "While the Continental architect considered it his task to make the fronts of the building as imaginative as possible, the English endeavoured to let them express what had to be said in the simplest and most concise way". Nevertheless, these plain, understated exteriors often concealed lavish interiors with elaborate ornamental plasterwork and joinery.

One of the characteristics of this city was the London square – terraces of individual houses set around a communal garden area for the private enjoyment of surrounding residents. As well as providing much needed green space, they created a distinctive urban grain which gave a unity to the city as a whole and linked the wealthiest with the poorest districts.

But there was another much more subtle reason for the remarkable cohesion of Georgian and early Victorian London, long since forgotten; a secret ingredient which conferred an innate harmony on the city, and which influenced everything from the layout of an entire neighbourhood to the size of a window pane – the Imperial system of measures.

Neighbourhoods were laid out by surveyors who used acres, furlongs, rods and chains – measurements which had been in common usage for marking out arable land since the 9th century. An acre was the length of a furlong (or furrow's length), 660ft, and its width was one chain, 66ft. For shorter lengths a perch, a pole or a rod were used. There were four rods to one chain. A London workman's house had a frontage of one rod or 16ft 6inches. In East London, one chain corresponded to four house frontages, so entire districts were created based on endogenous proportional relationships. The builders used rules divided into feet and inches, or fathoms (the length of outstretched arms), which meant that the actual proportions deployed for the construction of public spaces,

Above: 63–66 Grange Walk, Bermondsey, 29 April 1943. View of the rear elevation of a row of timber cottages c.1700. The lath and plaster can be seen clearly beneath the dilapidated weatherboarding. At first floor level are horizontal, sliding "Yorkshire" casements.

houses and their internal furnishings were derived directly from the human form, which accounts for their inherent unity. Covent Garden, for instance, was laid out as 6 x 5 chains and Belgrave Square as 10 x 10 chains, or 10 acres.

Thus the late Georgian/early Victorian city was infused by a common system of harmonious proportions, from the layout of an entire area to the pattern of its paving. Much of the subsequent development of London saw the fragmentation of this unified whole – with the coming of the railways, road widening, metropolitan improvements and the construction of larger buildings on aggregated plots for a whole variety of new uses. Nevertheless, a great deal of this urban backcloth remains in areas such as Islington, Bloomsbury, Hackney, Camberwell and Lambeth.

As London expanded relentlessly outwards from its bi-polar centres in the City of London and Westminster, it embraced and later subsumed older village cores and outlying areas, many of which retained rural and vernacular buildings, normally associated with a rural idyll, surviving well into the 20th century; Rotherhithe, with its weatherboarded cottages, had a greater affinity with the fishing villages of the Thames Estuary than the great maw of London.

Timber remained a common building material for smaller Georgian houses until well into the mid 18th century, particularly near the river where there was a ready supply of timber from the wharves and warehouses serving the Baltic and North American trade. Sometimes this was concealed behind brick facades, but often houses were fully weatherboarded. Rare today, many survived into the 20th century, as can be discerned in the photographs of

Bermondsey, Rotherhithe, Lambeth and Limehouse. In these outlying areas, there was a creative intermingling of the urban tradition of "polite" architecture with long-established rural vernacular traditions, which reached into town from the east along the river and from the surrounding Home Counties.

In the poorer areas, away from estate control, development pressures were intense as speculative builders vied to cram as many fifth-rate dwellings into as small a space as possible. The result was the sort of housing which can be seen at Bankside and across many parts of the East End, with families densely packed into tight networks of sunless courts and blind alleys, sharing communal privies, with a single tap or pump providing (frequently contaminated) water for an entire parish. A handful of the more fortunate lived in charitable almshouses erected by City livery companies, or local parishes for the deserving poor.

In the mid-19th century urban life was a nightmare for the poorer classes. Until the "Sanitary Idea", promoted by reformers such as Edwin Chadwick and Southwood Smith, began to make headway in the 1850s, the concept of environmental health was as alien to Victorian minds as the connection between dirt and disease. Cholera was thought to be a miasmatic vapour transmitted by foul air. Dustheaps and middens the size of four-storey houses attracted scavengers or "bunters" who made a living by reclaiming anything of value. The largest, a huge dustheap at King's Cross, was the setting for Noddy Boffin's business in Dickens' *Our Mutual Friend*.

By 1900, after 50 years of metropolitan improvements and sanitary reform, some of the worst nuisances of the previous decades had been addressed, but poverty was still endemic and life expectancy much lower for the indigent poor. In 1850 in London the average life expectancy at birth was 38 years compared with the national average of 41. By 1890 it had risen to 44 compared with 46 nationally, but these figures concealed terrible differentials. In 1900 a person in the West End had twice the life expectancy of a person in the East End. The average age at death in the West End was 55. In the East End it was 30. Childhood mortality rates were even more shocking. In the West End 18 per cent of children died before the age of 5; in the East End 55 per cent. In some streets, Jack London noted "out of every hundred children born in a year, fifty-five die before they are five years old".

The construction of new bridges in the early 19th century opened up new areas south of the river for development beyond the ancient centres of Borough and Lambeth. Here was London's service area, lined with a chaotic jumble of wharves, warehouses and noxious industries; dark canyons separated by slit-like alleys leading to river stairs and jetties. Many, such as those in Shad Thames, Bermondsey and Rotherhithe, still survive, converted into stylish loft apartments, demonstrating the innate versatility and sustainability of so much of London's historic fabric.

Above: Helmet Court, 11 June 1906: For centuries, the north side of the Strand was characterised by a whole series of narrow, mediaeval passages and courts, a handful of which can still be found towards the west end. Helmet Court stood just to the north and west of Somerset House. The narrow whitewashed entrance to the Strand can be seen in the distance.

Particular areas were distinguished by their smells. Bermondsey, for instance, was rank with the smell of leather tanning, breweries and vinegar vats.

There is no doubt at all that the growth of the early conservation movement was driven by a reaction against the massive scale of the changes that were transforming late-19th-century London into a great imperial and commercial capital and at the wholesale destruction of old buildings that accompanied it. Successive waves of railway construction from 1836 onwards, compounded later by the underground railway, cut huge swathes through the metropolis. Increasingly, the repetitive terraces of the 18th- and 19th-century city, that had once imparted such a remarkable unity to the capital, were being scythed through by massive waves of reconstruction.

With the relentless expansion of London's population, major metropolitan improvements cut further swathes through some of London's most historic neighbourhoods. In the City of London, Cannon Street had been widened as early as the 1850s, but later improvements were even more radical. In the 1860s a whole series of new thoroughfares were driven through the Cities of London and Westminster. Queen Victoria Street radically altered the geometry and grain of the City of London; the creation of Holborn Viaduct and

Farringdon Street transformed the entire morphology of the area between the City of London and the poorer districts to the west around Hatton Garden and, triggered by the colossal metropolitan market improvements at Smithfield, one of the greatest exercises of Victorian civic improvement ever seen in Britain – a massive, multi-layered complex of grand new market buildings designed by the City Surveyor, Sir Horace Jones– was superimposed over a network of subterranean railways.

The momentum of civic improvement continued remorselessly. Proposals for a major new road between Holborn and the Strand came to fruition in 1905. They entailed the comprehensive redevelopment of a huge area, the eviction of over 3,700 people and the eradication of one of London's worst slums around Drury Lane and Clare Market. These were photographed systematically as the entire neighbourhood was reconfigured for the formation of the great new commercial boulevards of Kingsway and Aldwych, which over the next twenty years were lined with majestic classical buildings reflecting the commercial might of the British Empire. In the process, some of inner London's most historic areas were destroyed completely. Among the most

grievous losses was the clearance of Holywell Street and Wych Street, regarded as the most picturesque in London, and which contained one of the finest concentrations of pre-Fire houses in the capital. Today, only the erroneously named Old Curiosity Shop, No. 13 Portsmouth Street, and a sole survivor – the White Horse public house in Clements Inn Passage – predate the Edwardian improvements.

In the City and West End, large areas of central London were reconstructed in grand Edwardian Beaux Arts style in a magnificent expression of civic pride and commercial and imperial self-confidence. In the City vast new citadels were raised for commerce, banking and insurance. The massive, forbidding hulk of Newgate Prison was demolished for the spectacular new Central Criminal Courts in 1903. Even the old Christ's Hospital, a City institution for over 300 years, succumbed when it was relocated to Horsham and its site redeveloped.

As the pace of change quickened, the preservation of historic buildings began to be seen as a popular cause for the educated middle-classes, and as an integral part of the emerging interest in town planning and philanthropy. In 1879 William Morris founded the Society for the Protection of Ancient Buildings (SPAB) "to keep watch on old monuments" and "to protect against all 'restoration' that means more than keeping out wind and weather".

In 1889 The London Topographical Society was formed. In 1893–95 Octavia Hill, Robert Hunter and Canon Hardwicke Rawnsley, a keen amateur photographer, founded the National Trust for Places of Historic Interest and Natural Beauty, which drew together interest in protecting landscapes with enthusiasm for preserving historic buildings. It attracted 250 members in its first year. Initially, the Trust worked with private companies to help keep historic buildings in use. The restoration of Staple Inn by the Prudential Assurance Company under the watchful eye of the SPAB was an early success.

Growing public unease at both the scale and pace of change was expressed both in the press and in parliamentary committees, but in 1893 the demolition of the finest building in East London – the old Royal Palace at Bromley-by-Bow – for a London County Council (LCC) Board School provoked widespread comment. In exasperation at the unthinking and unplanned destruction of so much of London's architectural heritage, a group of private individuals came together to form the London Survey Committee with the primary aim of recording buildings before they were destroyed.

The work of the London Survey Committee was hugely important for the growth of the conservation movement. Increasingly, preservation was identified with progressive planning and utilitarian ideals rather than just whimsical antiquarianism. The preservation of historic buildings, parks and open spaces was seen as an integral part of a wider social idealism – the provision of the proper amenities of life for a great city and for adequate housing for the poor; a concept taken up and given substance in the Utopian visions which underpinned the new Garden Suburbs, which were being built on the fringes of London at Brentham, Hampstead, Ealing and elsewhere.

The Survey Committee soon worked in close partnership with the LCC. Subsequently, it was absorbed into the LCC, and much later it became the Greater London Council (GLC) Historic Buildings Committee. With the abolition of the GLC in 1984, the old GLC Historic Buildings Division and its Historic Buildings Committee were united with the newly formed English Heritage. The London Advisory Committee of English Heritage continues this valuable role today. Over 100 years since its creation, it still provides advice on all major development affecting London's historic environment.

From 1900 to 1914 London underwent a public transport revolution that facilitated the development of outlying areas into new residential suburbs. The electrification of the railways and tramways, and the development of the deep tube and bus network precipitated major population shifts. In the

10 years from 1901 over 55,000 people, 12 per cent of the population, migrated from inner London, most to the new suburbs. Journeys on public transport virtually doubled over the same period from 142 to 250 per head of population.

With the outbreak of the First World War, shortages of both labour and supplies torpedoed many of London's Edwardian "grands projets". The reconstruction of Regent Street, Kingsway and County Hall ground to a halt, together with most new house building when, in 1916, all new building was proscribed under the Defence of the Realm Act.

In the period following the First World War, rising land values, population growth and the demands of the car generated intense commercial pressures for new development and further waves of metropolitan improvements. The pre-war momentum for new buildings for a new age re-emerged with even greater vigour as department stores, cinemas, commercial buildings, government offices and blocks of flats transformed the face of the capital.

By 1927 the population of London had reached 7,800,000, an increase of 20 per cent in just 25 years fuelled by the expansion of the public transport network. The first bus stops arrived in the 1920s and buses with roofs were introduced in 1925. The extension of a sophisticated network of buses and electric tramways facilitated the development of new outlying areas like East Sheen, Wimbledon, Kingston and Teddington, whilst the radical expansion of the underground and surface railways generated unprecedented opportunities for further suburban growth. In 1921, Dagenham, for example, was a struggling parish on the eastern fringe of London with a population of less than 10,000. In six years it had grown into a town of 50,000 with "homes fit for heroes" to live in.

In the inter-war years the height, massing and bulk of central London underwent a step-change. Many were apoplectic at the changes. Having celebrated London as "The Unique City", the Dane Steen Eiler Rasmussen castigated the introduction of continental experiments and ideas, which he believed were unsuited to London's character, particularly the replacement of conventional London streets with large estates of flats for public housing. Inter-war residential development was shaped by powerful centrifugal forces. Between 1921 and 1938 almost 200,000 people were displaced from central and inner London by slum clearance projects and Council housing programmes. Most never returned to their old neighbourhoods where large blocks of Council flats replaced the terraced houses, yards and alleys of Victorian London, dispersing many old communities in a Cockney diaspora. Waves of successive migration pushed people out from the centre into the inner ring, which, in turn, eroded the cohesion of middle-class communities, who moved out to the suburbs.

By 1939 the population of Greater London was 8.2 million – well ahead of New York with 6.93 million. It was not just the largest city in the world, it was its largest port, handling twice the tonnage of Liverpool. It was the seat of

Above: Albert Buildings, 39–53 Queen Victoria Street, 1899
Built in 1871 by F J Ward and occupying a triangular island site, the
main elevations of Albert Buildings are formed as elegant Italian
Gothic arcades, which run continuously around the bull-nosed
corners. Faced in painted stone, the fifth floor central section to
Queen Victoria Street forms a sheer attic storey with an elaborate
machicolated cornice and parapet. The building remains much the
same today with shops at street level and offices above.

government, the monarchy and the judiciary. It was the
cosmopolitan capital of the British Empire at the moment of
its greatest extent. It financed half the world's trade, while
the volume of its manufacturing output exceeded that of any
of the great industrial conurbations of the Midlands and the
North. It was the focal point of the road and rail network;
the primary cultural centre with many of the leading
museums and galleries of the age containing world-famous
collections. London was the pre-eminent world city, the
dynamo that powered Britain and widely acknowledged to
be the finest city in the world. But with one-fifth of Britain's
population concentrated into just 610 sq miles, by 1939
London was also a shockingly vulnerable target.

Today it is difficult to comprehend the scale of wartime
destruction. In one night alone, on Sunday, 29 December
1940, the City of London lost about a third of its entire
floorspace. The ensuing fire, which could be seen 30 miles
away, leapt the river and ignited a line of warehouses on the
south bank between London Bridge and Tower Bridge.
Almost every building between Moorgate and Aldersgate
Street was obliterated, including the ancient maze of streets
and alleys around Paternoster Row in the shadow of St Paul's.
Over 6 million books burned in the flames. Tragically, old
buildings were the most vulnerable. While modern
steel-framed buildings withstood high explosives and fire
relatively well, older masonry structures simply collapsed.

By the end of the war the level of damage was truly
shocking, 50,000 houses destroyed or irreparable in inner
London alone, and over 60,000 in outer London. An additional
290,000 houses suffered serious damage and a further
2 million or more slight damage.

A whole series of factors determined the form and pattern
of post-war reconstruction – not least radical idealism
coupled with an unprecedented opportunity to create a
socially engineered New Jerusalem. With the exception of
major landmark buildings, in the headlong rush to embrace
the future there was little appetite for retaining the past.
Whole streets of perfectly serviceable, but damaged, houses
were left to rot by speculative developers, or abandoned by
local authorities determined to build a fairer and more socially
just society. In many parts of inner London and the East End,
the opportunity was seized to clear large areas of insanitary
and sub-standard housing in a concerted effort to improve
social conditions. As a result, even greater damage was

inflicted on historic areas which had survived the Luftwaffe, through comprehensive redevelopment, particularly in the poorer areas of inner and east London – at King Square, Finsbury, for instance, or Bromley-by-Bow, which was virtually wiped off the map by an unholy alliance of comprehensive redevelopment and massive new highway engineering.

However, there were some who stood against the tide of comprehensive redevelopment in favour of a more delicate form of urban surgery and place-making. Many of the great architectural set-pieces such as Buckingham Palace and the Palace of Westminster were repaired with painstaking authenticity. The landed estates of the West End which exercised freehold control – the Crown, Grosvenor, Portman, Bedford and Howard de Walden for instance, took a much longer and more enlightened view of their stewardship. By and large they carefully stitched back the damaged fabric of their buildings and streets to their pre-war appearance.

Today it is possible to walk from the Embankment through Inner and Middle Temple, past Street's magnificent Law Courts, through Lincoln's Inn, across High Holborn to Gray's Inn and beyond into Bloomsbury and still appreciate their historic qualities The primary reason for this was the unfashionable approach adopted by the privately-owned Inns in insisting upon recreating the qualities which made a place special – based on a deep understanding that the importance of the place transcended the sum of its component parts. This was achieved in the face of intense opposition by local authorities, and of scorn from the modernist architectural establishment of the day, who strongly favoured sweeping the past away for comprehensive redevelopment. Yet with the benefit of hindsight, who was more progressive in their approach to placemaking?

Britain now leads the world in the sophistication of its mechanisms for managing change to its historic environment. One of the reasons London has become so successful is that public pressure has brought about a much better balance between continuity and change which, in turn, has enhanced the capital's appeal to overseas investors and visitors. Londoners care passionately about the places where they live as much as individual buildings. Increasingly, historic buildings are seen as an asset, not a constraint on progress. They command a premium in the open market, and, at a time when it is imperative to reduce carbon emissions, it is recognised that the creative reuse of old buildings is inherently sustainable, reutilising the embodied energy they contain. Routinely, warehouses, tenements, factories and other old buildings are being adapted, converted and reused by developers who have realised, at last, that history sells and a better way to build the New Jerusalem lies in the imaginative recycling of those "dark satanic mills".

Top: 10 Carlton House Terrace, 6 May 1942. View of 10 Carlton House Terrace immediately to the east of Duke of York's Steps. The attic storey has been blown off and the stucco facades are pitted by shrapnel.

Middle: St Mary, Aldermanbury, 20 March 1941. View of the gutted shell of the Wren church and the surviving Corinthian columns that divided the nave and aisles. The ruins were dismantled and shipped to Fulton, Missouri.

Above: 2 Great Cumberland Place, Marylebone, November 1928. A demolished corner plot at the junction with Oxford Street with huge raking shores propping the adjacent houses. To the right are the offices of Dunkley Prams.

WORK

London is built on commerce and trade; an economic constant that echoes across generations. In the first half of the 20th century London was indisputably the world's greatest metropolis; the cosmopolitan capital of the British Empire at the moment of its greatest extent. It financed half the world's trade, but was also the world's largest workshop and its greatest port. It was the focal point of its road and rail network with an intricate web of transport links radiating from the pulsating heart of the capital. But it was also the country's primary cultural centre with a spectacular concentration of museums and galleries containing world-famous collections from all quarters of the globe.

In 1910 London lay unchallenged as the pre-eminent world city; the economic dynamo that powered Britain and its Empire. A hundred years later, in spite of the vicissitudes of the global economy, if London were a country it would rank within the top 15 world economies with a GVA (Gross Value Added) greater than that of Switzerland or Saudi Arabia. Together with New York and Tokyo, London remains one of three world cities, and arguably it is still the greatest.

In 1901 40 per cent of its workforce was employed in manufacturing and 60 per cent in retail, transport and the construction industry. Over the previous century a sinuous ribbon of wharves, warehouses and workshops lined the Thames and its tributaries; a chaotic agglomeration of timber yards, ships' chandlers, copper and lead works, generating stations, breweries and factories. London was also the country's main manufacturing centre with a worldwide reputation for quality and excellence and an industrial output that exceeded that of Manchester, Birmingham, Liverpool or Glasgow.

The docks were the largest single employer, but by 1900 cut-throat competition had pushed many dock companies to the brink of collapse. Nine years later they were subsumed into the new Port of London Authority, which regulated dock labour and regenerated London's maritime trade from its palatial new headquarters in Trinity Square, the construction of which necessitated the clearance of a whole district around Savage Gardens and Trinity Square.

Until the 1960s, with the advent of containerisation and their relocation down river, the produce of the world poured through London Docks – tea, cocoa and coffee; sugar, ivory, silk and tobacco; softwoods from the Baltic, hardwoods from Africa, exotic fruits from the colonies, grain and cattle from Canada and refrigerated meat from Argentina and Uruguay. As late as the 1970s the cavernous riverside warehouses of Wapping and Southwark were laced with the pungent aroma of nutmeg, cinnamon, cardamom and camphor from the tropics.

London's great strength lay in the extraordinary diversity of its economic base – paramount not just in manufacturing and trade, but in commerce and international financial services too. In 1911 Charles Booth wrote "London is supreme not only in variety, but in total magnitude". The great shipping, insurance and banking houses of the City managed Britain's vast overseas investments from magnificent temples of commerce which increasingly replaced the older domestic-scaled buildings of the 18th and 19th centuries.

In 1851 the resident population of the City of London had been 129,000, many of whom were shopkeepers, craftsmen, tailors and artisans. A great deal of manufacturing still took place over the shop and in small backyard factories and workshops, but by 1901 its population had shrunk to 27,000. Many small traders and craftsmen migrated to the City fringe, or to new, purpose-built premises in the Lea Valley, Park Royal and the expanding suburbs. By 1905 four-fifths of the entire City had been rebuilt in the past 50 years, doubling the amount of floorspace for banks, insurance companies, shipping agents and brokers, who oiled the wheels of global and imperial commerce. The City's residential population was replaced by armies of office workers, who commuted daily via the great railway termini, on the underground, and later the deep tube.

Across London teeming neighbourhoods of high-density housing supported large numbers of local shops, home-based businesses and sweated trades in small local workshops and backyards. Over 20,000 young women were employed as casual seamstresses in the fashion houses and tailoring shops of Soho and the West End to cater for the sartorial whims of high society. London's myriad urban villages fostered particular clusters of manufacturing activity – furniture-making in Shoreditch, leather in Bermondsey, pianos in Camden Town, jewellery in Hatton Garden, clothing in Soho, East Marylebone and Whitechapel, second-hand cloth and paper around Smithfield, and printing and publishing around St Paul's – as older trades like ship-building and silk-weaving declined. As late as the Second World War, there were around 40,000 factories in inner London employing over 740,000 people. All of this was connected and serviced by a vast transport network of haulage contractors, carmen, and costermongers who provided the lifeblood of the capital and who can be seen in the photographs going about their daily business.

Opposite: London Bridge, c.1900: A view from the south-west, looking towards the Church of St Magnus the Martyr with the Monument behind and to its left. All the traffic is horse drawn, while shipping is drawn up alongside the warehouses to the right.

Urban workshops

Left: 13 & 14 Archer Street, Soho, 20 May 1908
The upper floors of many Soho houses were given over to workshops, often serving the larger West End stores, particularly the rag trade. In this case, the two women are engaged in upholstery and trimming for the furniture trade.

Below: Denmark Place, St Giles's, c.1908
Denmark Place is a narrow passage behind the north side of Denmark Street, which housed a range of small workshops. Behind No. 27 was a blacksmith's forge. The back of the forge chimney is not bonded to the wall to minimise the risk of fire.

Above: 223 Bow Road, 19 November 1909

M Howes was an old established corn and flour dealer selling animal feed, horse mixture, straw and hay from a double-bay 17th-century house. Marooned by the post-war Bow flyover, remarkably the building still exists; one of the oldest in the East End.

**Above (left and right):
Apothecaries Hall, Blackfriars Lane,
16 November 1911**

View of the Still Room (above left) and
the huge central grindstones used in the
preparation of medicines. Apothecaries
Hall dates from 1684 and was altered in
1779. Although the livery hall was the
grand formal function room of the guild,
medicines and pharmaceutical products
were also prepared here for public use.

**Left: 210 New Kings Road, Fulham,
c.1945**

Richard Dwight was granted a patent for
the manufacture of pottery and ceramics
in 1672, and for over 250 years Fulham
Pottery was an industrial site at the west
end of New Kings Road. The site was
redeveloped in 1979–80 but a 19th-
century bottle kiln, with its characteristic
domed profile, was retained. It can still
be seen alongside the new office block.

**Above: 26 Steward Street,
Stepney, 20 November 1944**
War damage meant that business
often continued from semi-
derelict buildings. In some
districts of London it was difficult
to find a single house with
unbroken windows.

**Right: 48–50 Aldgate,
27 September 1908**
The butchers and eel shops which
occupied this group of buildings
provided produce to nearby City
restaurants.

Legal precincts

Clifford's Inn, 1903

Named after Robert de Clifford, who was granted the property by Edward II, an independent Inn was established by law students in 1345 and affiliated to the Inner Temple. The entire Inn was sold in 1903, when these photographs were taken, but it remained occupied until its demolition in 1935. Only the gateway survives.

Above left: Early-18th-century lawyers' chambers and the western end of the hall, built in 1767. The original hall escaped the Great Fire. The Judges of the Great Fire Court met there in 1670 to resolve rebuilding disputes between landlords and tenants.

Top right: 10, 12 & 13 Clifford's Inn, 1903
View showing the passageway through to Serjeants Inn, Chancery Lane, and the beautifully textured courtyard surface in natural stone.

Above: Great Scotland Yard, 3 November 1906
A police station was established here in 1829. It became the Metropolitan Police headquarters until 1891 when it relocated to New Scotland Yard.

City streets

Right: London Bridge, c.1880
Heavily laden horse-drawn carts cross London Bridge. At the beginning of the 19th century the mediaeval bridge was becoming so congested that a competition was launched to design a replacement. John Rennie's design was selected and his five-arched stone bridge was opened in 1831.

Below: Bank of England, Threadneedle Street, c.1895
A corner view of the original Bank of England building with pedestrians and horse-drawn vehicles in the foreground. The building was constructed by Sir John Soane in 1788 on a three-and-a-half-acre site, but later extensively rebuilt between 1923-39 by Sir Herbert Baker, retaining Soane's outer perimeter screen.

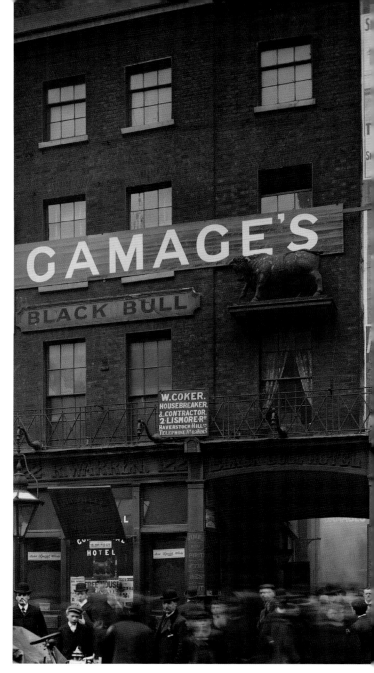

Coaching inns and gin palaces

Above: The Black Bull Inn, Holborn, 8 April 1904
The Black Bull was a well-known coaching inn. It was here that Sarah Gamp and Betsey Prig nursed Mr Lewsome in Dickens' *Martin Chuzzlewit*. The figure of the bull over the main entrance was modelled for William Lockwood, the inventor of Portland cement. On demolition for the new Gamages Department store, it was relocated to the offices of Sir William Bull MP in King Street, Hammersmith.

Above left: The Old Bell Tavern and Hotel, Holborn, c.1897: Situated next to the Black Bull, The Old Bell, was another renowned coaching inn.

Opposite: The Leicester, Leicester Square, c.1905
The Leicester, on the corner of Wardour Street at the junction with Leicester Square, was renowned for its spectacular ornamental ironwork. A battery of angled mirrors can be seen in the passageway to the left to improve the daylighting.

Top left: The opulent lounge bar on the first floor.

Above: Whitehall Gardens, 1 May 1912
Whitehall Gardens, formerly Privy Gardens, lay at
the rear of the Banqueting House and was lined with
fashionable mansions which, until the formation of the
Victoria Embankment, had gardens and lawns sloping
down to the Thames.

Malmesbury House to the left of the picture was
built in the 1720s and once faced the rear of the
Banqueting House. From 1834–61 it was the house
of James Howard, 3rd Earl of Malmesbury, Foreign
Secretary and later Leader of the House of Lords. The
Ionic entrance screen adjacent is the entrance lodge to
Pembroke House, one of the first Palladian villas, built
in 1724 and later altered by Sir William Chambers in
1757. Whitehall Gardens was levelled in 1936 for a huge
new building for the Air Ministry and Board of Trade,
now the Ministry of Defence.

**Left: Pembroke House, 7 Whitehall Gardens,
23 September 1912**
Pembroke House was renowned for its exquisite
plasterwork by William Parfitt to designs by Sir William
Chambers. This view shows Room 24 on the first floor
with its superb spider's web ceiling with an entwining
vine encircled by a large rope of fruit and flowers.
Room 24 and three others from Pembroke House were
reassembled in the new Ministry building.

Whitehall

**Left: 2 Whitehall Gardens,
22 May 1912**
2 Whitehall Gardens was used by the Cabinet Office and the Committee of Imperial Defence. The first floor rear room was treated in a French rococo style with oil paintings of rural scenes painted by E J Parris in 1841.

Below: Waterloo Place, c.1900
Looking south towards the Duke of York Column on a misty winter's day. The equestrian statue of Field Marshal Napier (replaced in the 1920s by one of Edward VII) is immediately to the north and the Guards' Crimean Monument is also prominent.

Covent Garden

Above: Bedford Chambers,
Covent Garden, 26 September 1921
Built between 1629 and 1637 to the design of Inigo Jones, Covent Garden was the first square to be laid out in London. By the late 18th century, the buildings had been progressively redeveloped. Bedford Chambers, 1877–79 by Henry Clutton, echoed Jones's original design. The lamp standard to the left marked the entrance to an underground public convenience for market traders in the basement of Thomas Archer's once magnificent Baroque mansion of 1716–17 built for Admiral

Russell. The arched gable of the Floral Hall can be seen in the distance with the top of its original dome just above the roofline.

Opposite above: Bedford Chambers,
Covent Garden, 26 September 1921
The view from within the arcade of Bedford Chambers towards King Street is little altered today. The Great Western Railway had a receiving office here. Note the impressive phalanx of brass plates by the door to the right.

**Below: Floral Hall,
Covent Garden, c.1925**
London's markets were the
bustling trading centres of
the city, spawning a rich and
vigorous sub-culture offering
produce from across the world
– here, pears, plums and apples
from Australia. Built between
1858–60 by E M Barry in pre-
fabricated cast-iron, the Floral
Hall broke into the main Piazza
with an arched elevation. The
eastern part was restored in
1997–99 as part of the Royal
Opera House development.
The arched frontage to the
Piazza was dismantled and later
reconstructed as part of Borough
Market.

Above: 225 Oxford Street, 2 January 1908
John Bell & Co. traded from this delightful late-18th-century shopfront for over a century before amalgamating with Croyden & Co. and relocating to Wigmore Street. The building was redeveloped in 1909 for the London Cinematograph Co., later the home of the Studio One and Studio Two cinemas.

Left: 7 George Street, Marylebone Lane, c.1906
A fine late-18th-century shopfront with leaded fanlights, a shallow curved window subdivided by glazing bars, and a raised and fielded panelled entrance door to the upper floors.

Shops and markets

Above: Earlham Street, Seven Dials, 17 August 1908

The north side of Earlham Street looking east towards Seven Dials. London was once renowned for the spontaneity of its street life and the vibrancy of its street markets, many of which have now vanished. Exuberant iron lanterns carried on massive ornamental brackets were a common feature of the townscape. The three buildings to the left survive.

Right: 98-102 High Street, Fulham, 6 May 1904

A view once redolent of many parts of the inner suburbs: a mixed group of 18th-century domestic buildings housing a range of local traders – hair-cutting rooms, cobblers, a steam cycle works and sweet shop. The entire group was demolished for an extension of the LCC's tramway track from Hammersmith to Putney Bridge in 1909.

Serving the grand houses

**Left: Woburn Buildings,
2–14 Dukes Road, Euston, c.1920**
Woburn Buildings remains one of London's most picturesque places. Built to serve the grand houses on the adjacent Bedford Estate, they form part of Thomas Cubitt's original design of 1822 with a beautiful sequence of curved bay windows to the shops. Milk and fresh farm produce were brought into the great railway stations daily; hence the line of milk churns on the footway, which still retains the original massive York stone slabs over the cellars beneath.

Below: 3 Houghton Street, c.1906
The late 19th century was the heyday of ornamental signwriting before the advent of neon. H. West occupied this fine bowed shopfront with decorative Ionic columns to the entrance and fluted Greek pilasters to the window. To the right is the narrow entrance to Clare Passage.

Soho streets

Above: 6 New Compton Street, St Giles, c.1905
Dolman & Son were carvers and frame makers which might account for this spectacular Jacobean-style frontage with its intricately carved glazing bars and riot of ornamental detail. Its provenance is a mystery.

Right: 51–52 Frith Street, c.1905
Built in 1805 as two houses over a shop and manufactory, Nos. 51–52 Frith Street had elaborate rococo cast iron guard rails to the first floor windows over an imposing shopfront embellished with lions' heads and patterned fanlights.

Leather Lane

Opposite: Leather Lane, Holborn, 1891
A group of workmen standing on the pavement during the re-fit of a shop at the junction of Beauchamp Street and Leather Lane.

Right: 4–6 Houghton Street, 21 May 1906
The Aldwych Wire Works has a fine Georgian shopfront with an ornamental wire anchor hanging from the front. A pair of cats haunt the entrance next door.

Below: 56 Artillery Lane, Spitalfields, 12 November 1908
The finest surviving mid-Georgian shopfront in London in use as a grocers and general store. The entire frontage is divided into four bays of different widths by Doric three-quarter columns with iron grilles beneath the flat-fronted shop windows, which have curved corner bays. Above is a later elegant Regency balcony.

The royal tobacconist

Left: 34 Haymarket, 7 December 1908
Fribourg and Treyer, purveyors of snuff
and tobacco, began trading in 1751 and
closed in 1977. The delightful bow-fronted
shopfront, the oldest in London, with its
separate side entrance to the upper floors
and wrought iron grilles, still survives
as a gift shop, but it has lost much of its
original character.

Below: View of the shop interior and
fittings looking towards the street.

Liberty & Co.

Above: Regent Street, 1898
View of the Regent Street frontage of East India House, the premises of Liberty & Co and the silverware retailers, Mappin Brothers. Liberty, opened to the public in 1875, was in the vanguard of Arts & Crafts design, particularly in dress and home decoration.

Right: Euston Road, Camden, 1912
View of the 'Royal Blue' horse omnibus in front of numbers 5–7 Euston Road. The omnibus carries route information and advertisements for Selfridge's. The shops behind, including Boots the Chemist and the Northumberland Hotel, are also swathed in advertisements.

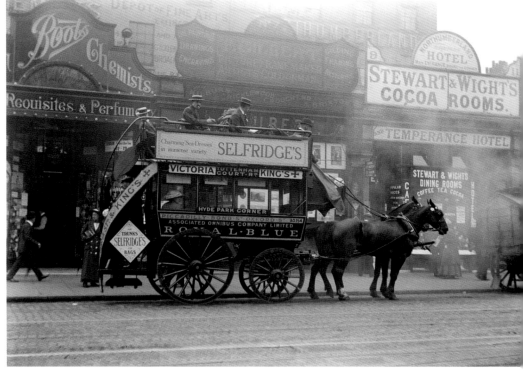

Below: 153-167 Regent Street, 8 August 1912
View of the west side south of New Burlington Street showing the elaborate ironwork over Hudson Bay House, the International Fur Store, and a battery of royal warrants over shopfronts.

Right: 29 Regent Street, c.1910
A splendid pair of bowed shopfronts with coronets crowning the fascias and beautifully detailed timber shutters.

Millbank

Above: Nos. 17–25 Millbank Street, 11 April 1904
The east side of Millbank was a jumble of wharves,
jetties, and industrial buildings. In the centre of the
picture is John Bazley White & Bros, Cement Works,
with the Hovis Imperial Flour Mills beyond. In
between are earlier 18th- and 19th-century houses.
All were swept away for an extension of the Thames
embankment and Victoria Tower Gardens under the
Westminster Improvement Act 1900.

Right: 20–22 Millbank Street, 21 May 1906
Old printing press.

The fourth estate

Left: 109 Fleet Street, 24 March 1909
Dundee newspapers and the Woolgar & Roberts Press Cutting Agency advertise their presence. This extraordinary picture shows a much-altered 18th-century house with later sgraffito decoration to the facade subsumed within a grand new Baroque building. Note the pediment and entablatures awaiting completion hanging over the attic windows of the house beneath.

Below left: Sardinia Street, 11 June 1906
View looking east, showing Beaufort House Printing Works and a milk delivery cart in the foreground.

Below right: Sardinia Place, c.1906
The mud-choked street at the northern end of Sardinia Place.

London's library

Above left: 53–54 Paternoster Row looking west, 1908
To the north of St Paul's Churchyard was one of the great
centres of the English book trade. Stationers and text writers
sold religious and educational books as well as paternosters
and graces, hence the name. By the early 18th century the
book trade prevailed, supplanting mercers, silk and lace
merchants and tire-men who sold "top knots and other
dressings for the female head". The entire district was
destroyed by enemy action on the night of 29 December 1940,
along with six million books.

Here, the London Bible Warehouse, trading from a fine
18th-century house, continued a tradition of ecclesiastical
publishing which originated in the shadow of St Paul's in the
Middle Ages.

Above right: 278 Whitechapel Road, 4 October 1899
Straker's stationers with a magnificent array of gas lanterns
across the fascia. The entire upper floor is covered with incised
gilded panels advertising other branches.

Heroic railway engineering

Above: Liverpool Street Station, c.1905
A view from the south-west of the station, which was
completed in 1875 to the designs of Edward Wilson in a
Gothic style as the terminus of the Great Eastern Railway.
The scene is a mixture of horse-drawn cabs and passengers.

Opposite above: St Pancras Station, Euston Road, c.1895
Designed by W H Barlow and R M Ordish for the Midland
Railway Company, when the station opened in 1868 the span

of the parabolic iron vault of the train shed was the largest
in the world.

Opposite below: Midland Grand Hotel, Euston Road, c.1890
Designed by Sir George Gilbert Scott, and a masterpiece of
Victorian Gothic architecture, the completed hotel opened
in 1876, but by 1935 its reputation had declined and it
was closed and used as railway offices. In one of the most
ambitious and visionary conservation projects of the last
30 years, it was eventually fully restored as a five-star
luxury hotel and apartments and re-opened in 2011 as the
St Pancras Renaissance Hotel.

Bankside

Above: Bankside, 16 May 1912
View looking west from No. 46 towards the power station, warehouses and wharves which characterised an area once known as London's backyard. The house next to British Lion Wharf (No. 48 Bankside), which survives, was allegedly occupied by Sir Christopher Wren so he could watch St Paul's arising directly opposite. The setted road surface is littered with horse dung: a recurrent nuisance and health hazard.

Opposite top: Panorama of Bankside from the foreshore near Trig Lane Stairs in the City of London, 21 June 1912
In the centre is the generating station of the City Electric Light Company, behind which rise the chimneys of the South Metropolitan Gas Company all of which was swept away for the construction of Bankside Power Station in 1952.

To the left is a short terrace of early-18th-century houses – No. 48 Bankside is to the extreme left. Behind lay Moss's Alley and the poisonous warren of courts and yards. Cardinal Cap Alley still survives next to 48 Bankside.

Opposite middle: Upper Ground, Blackfriars, c.1912
The whole of the South Bank of the Thames was given over to wharves, warehouses and industry. To the left are the spans of Blackfriars Bridge. *The Arandora Star* was fated – sunk off the coast of Ireland on 2 July 1940 with heavy loss of life.

Opposite bottom: Lambeth Suspension Bridge, c.1865
The bridge was constructed across the River Thames between 1861 and 1862. In the foreground a crane unloads bricks from a barge onto a cart.

Southwark Fire Station

Top left: Southwark Fire Station, Southwark Bridge Road, c.1908
Police, fire and ambulance stations overtly expressed the ideals of public service and civic pride. Southwark Fire Station was one of the most impressive. The splendid Gothic range in the distance housed the HQ of the Metropolitan Fire Brigade, but it was damaged in the Blitz and later demolished. However, the adjacent Engine House and tower survive, together with an Arts & Crafts extension of 1911.

Middle left: Southwark Fire Station, c.1908
The Engine House with the Metropolitan Fire Brigade in all its glory ready for action with a horse-drawn appliance in the centre. The same bays are in use today inscribed above with the initials of the Metropolitan Fire Brigade, the Metropolitan Board of Works and the date 1878.

Bottom left: Southwark Fire Station, c.1910
Scaling ladder drill in the courtyard. In the background are parts of the workhouse building erected in 1777 for St Saviour's parish.

Below: Southwark Fire Station, 1908
The centre of operations; the telephone switchboard in the Watch Room.

Above: Holborn Viaduct, 1868
Labourers work on the construction of Holborn Viaduct.
Completed in 1869, it connected Holborn Street with Newgate
Street. The hoarding in the foreground advertises St Pancras
Station, opened in 1868.

Silk weavers

Left: 36 Crispin Street, 25 March 1909
An elegant Spitalfields mansion (c1713) with a subtle carved ogee shape cut into the brickwork over the central bay. A French Huguenot chapel once stood at the rear. The shop, which was added around 1800, was occupied by a glass and china merchant until its demolition in the 1920s.

Below right: 42 Alma Road, Bethnal Green
The weavers' houses of Bethnal Green were highly distinctive, often only one room deep, with irregular fenestration patterns and long horizontal weavers' lights. Good light was crucial for the delicate art of silk weaving and colour matching, but by 1909 silk weaving was in sharp decline. Here the revolving drums of the spreading out machine can be seen in operation.

Below left: 42 Alma Road, 24 May 1909
The front half of the same room showing spreading out machinery and hand looms.

Opposite: 17 Fleet Street, 1899
The north elevation of 17 Fleet Street, occupied by Carter's Hair Cutting Saloon, showing figures, including a policeman, gathered either side of the gateway to Inner Temple. This rare timber-framed survival was claimed to be the palace of Henry VIII and Cardinal Wolsey, as alleged on the advertising on the facade, but this was a popular urban myth. It was built as a tavern in 1610–11.

Borough High Street

Left: 146-154 Borough High Street, c.1905
For centuries, Borough High Street was the principal approach to the City of London from the south. It was lined with coaching inns and yards which conferred a very distinctive character.

These 17th century timber-framed houses were typical of the area. Chaplin's was a dealer in India rubber, gutta percha and protective clothing.

Below left: 142–154 Borough High Street, 20 September 1908
Nos. 142–144, with its distinctive parapet frieze of swags and bucrania, was designed by Sir John Soane. Through the central archway was a long, narrow passage lined with terraces and four semi-detached houses built for Francis Adams by Soane in 1785 – hence the inscribed panel over the entrance reading Adams Place. The name was altered later by some wag to Eve's Place.

Wretched remains...

Opposite below right: 189–191 Borough High Street, c.1903
A fine group of 17th-century timber-framed vernacular houses on the west side of the street. Many of the goods displayed were beyond the reach of the poorest classes, who were crammed into one of London's most notorious slums in the alleys and yards behind the High Street.

Above: 199a Borough High Street, 14 September 1908
Borough High Street served the wharves, warehouses and industries clustered along the Thames. Depicted here are the old drying sheds of a vat maker in Layton's Yard, later part of Layton & Young, of Young's brewery. The ancient cobbled road surface is probably part of the King's Bench Prison, which stood on the site and was demolished in 1758.

Billingsgate

Left: Billingsgate Market, 1905
A dockside view with porters crowding outside the entrance to Billingsgate Market. Rebuilt between 1874 and 1877 to designs by Sir Horace Jones, the French Renaissance facade cloaked a functional interior. The market moved from its Lower Thames Street site in 1982 to a new location on the Isle of Dogs, and the old market building was converted to an exhibition and events venue.

Above: Mabie, Todd and Company, 319–329 Weston Street, Southwark, 1913
A view of workers standing outside the warehouse at Mabie, Todd and Company, fountain pen manufacturers. This American firm became established in England in the 1880s and thrived until the era of ballpoint pens when production declined and it closed at the end of the 1950s.

Above: 216-224 Borough High Street, c.1905
No. 220 Borough High Street is an ancient timber-framed house given over with its neighbour to the production of domestic hardware and equipment.

Right: Albert Road, North Woolwich, 21 March 1899
The densely packed neighbourhoods of the East End supported large numbers of local shops catering for a whole range of daily needs. R Hodge was a general dealer stocking household provisions including cheese, bacon, vegetables, tea, chocolate and black fuel for coal fires.

WEALTH

The wealth created from generations of successful trade and enterprise was invested in buildings which exuded the power and status of their owners. Increasingly, the older merchants' houses of 18th-century London, like those in Spitalfields and the once fashionable houses of the aristocracy in the West End, gave way to a new wave of opulent buildings which reflected the rising wealth of the emerging industrial and middle classes.

Philanthropy is a rich, continuous seam permeating London's history. There is a long and noble tradition of wealthy benefactors providing endowments for the poor, the sick and the needy. One of its most tangible manifestations is the foundation of almshouses for the poor, where a lucky few enjoyed decent living conditions in small, sheltered communities. Morden College was a typical early example, whilst Thomas Coram's establishment of the Foundling Hospital in Bloomsbury in 1742 created a London institution which saved generations of abandoned children from abuse, starvation and premature death on the streets. The ancient City Livery Companies were particularly active in endowing almshouses and schools, using their great repositories of wealth for philanthropic ends. Many of the great livery halls in the City – like Drapers' Hall – were sumptuously enriched or rebuilt to proclaim the greater glory of their guild.

In the West End, the Freemasons went from strength to strength expanding on their site in Great Queen Street with a whole series of opulent buildings – all of which were swept away in 1927–32, including fine rooms by Sir John Soane and Philip Hardwick, for a colossal new headquarters with even more spectacular interiors by Ashley & Newman.

The surge of new development swept through the West End. The Ritz Hotel in Piccadilly, one of London's first steel-framed buildings, was completed in 1906 to the design of Mewès and Davis; while in St James's new discreetly grand gentlemen's clubs replaced the mansions of the aristocracy. The Royal Automobile Club displaced both Cumberland House and Buckingham House in 1911. The Savage Club, renowned for its bohemian antics, moved frequently; while older political institutions, like the Conservative Club, were solid bastions of the Establishment.

High society lived in a tightly defined area of Mayfair, St James's and Belgravia, where life for the social elite of around 7,000 people revolved around the Season opening on the Friday nearest 1 May with the Royal Academy Summer Exhibition and ending in late July after Goodwood. In between were the Derby, Ascot, the Chelsea Flower Show, Wimbledon and Henley, culminating in Queen Charlotte's Ball, where debutantes were presented at Court.

Some of the most lavish parties took place in the great aristocratic town houses of Mayfair – like Devonshire House, Dorchester House and Norfolk House, where the sons and daughters of the old landed families could be introduced socially to the new wealth of the industrial and commercial classes.

For the masses, the West End was London's playground – a glittering, vibrant world of the demi-monde, which offered illimitable opportunities for pleasure for all classes. The primary focus of this was around Piccadilly Circus, the heart of the Empire and the hub of London's louche nightlife. The Criterion restaurant was one of London's largest, its dining room famed throughout the world.

Increasingly, the expanding middle classes developed their own style – often wildly idiosyncratic, like William Burges's mediaeval Gothic fantasy, Tower House, in Kensington, built for his own use between 1876 and 1878.

Alongside the more overt expressions of new-found wealth, power remained deeply engrained in many of the older centres. Admiralty House and the Admiralty, with its extraordinary Board Room, remains celebrated as the scene of many of the most momentous events in British naval history. The Royal Institution for the Advancement of Science, founded in 1799, remains in the forefront of national intellectual life, while St James's Palace is still the official residence of the monarch and the court at which Ambassadors pay homage.

As the centrifugal forces driving London's expansion gathered momentum, the once-isolated mansions and villas of the wealthy were subsumed into the great maw; sometimes, like Belsize Lodge as islands marooned in a sea of new development, but, with rising land values, others like the haunting Gothic Hall in Highgate Road, succumbed to the relentless march of new development.

Opposite: 3 Lincoln's Inn Fields, 1911
The old library and dining room of the Sir John Soane museum.

Extensive clearance

Opposite above: Aldwych, 1913
Looking west from St Clement Danes Church towards the vacant corner site being developed for Australia House. The development of Aldwych, begun in 1905, was still in progress, as illustrated by the empty sites. On the incomplete gable wall is an advert encouraging emigration to Australia.

Opposite below: Waldorf Hotel, 11–43 Aldwych, 1901
The building site in front of the Hotel is all that remains of Wych Street and Drury Court, cleared to make way for the new Kingsway and Aldwych developments.

Above and left: St Clement Danes Church, 22 July 1905
The spectacular nave and apse showing Wren's lavish original plasterwork and the magnificent original 17th-century carved oak pulpit. The church was gutted by fire in 1941 and restored in 1955–58 by Anthony Lloyd.

Below: Mansion House Street, 1910
View along Mansion House Street towards the
Royal Exchange with the side elevation of the
Mansion House to the right. Between is the Royal
Insurance Building, built the year this photograph
was taken. The offices of the Equitable Life
Assurance Society are to the left.

Left and above: National Provincial Bank, Bishopsgate, c.1900
The former National Provincial Bank, designed by John Gibson in 1864–65, epitomised the swaggering commercial confidence of the mid-Victorian city. Crowned by allegorical statuary, the superb single-storey frontage is divided into equal bays by refined fluted Corinthian columns with carved panels of relief between. The frontage and main banking hall were retained as part of the wider redevelopment of the site for Tower 42 (the former National Westminster Tower) designed by Richard Seifert in 1970.

Above: The sumptuous interior with red marble columns and friezes of relief sculpture beneath three huge glass domes which flood the banking hall with light. The former banking hall is now a hospitality and conference venue.

Opulence

Above: 76 High Holborn, c.1912
Henry Treadwell and Leonard Martin were responsible for a
wonderfully inventive series of London buildings which were
a cocktail of Tudor, Baroque and Art Nouveau styles. James
Buchanan's, whiskey distillers, completed in 1909, was typical
of their effervescent mixture of styles. Sadly, the building was
destroyed in the Second World War.

Right: Freemasons' Hall,
Great Queen Street, Holborn, 15 March 1911
Founded in 1717, the Grand Lodge of England acquired a house
in Great Queen Street in 1774, triggering a complex series of
developments of ever-increasing grandeur. Two years later Thomas
Sandby designed the first purpose-built masonic hall in England
in the form of a Roman Doric temple enriched with masonic
symbols. The Anti-Slavery society was founded here in 1807,
and in 1863 the Football Association met for the first time in the
tavern at the front. Severely damaged by fire in 1883, Sandby's hall
survived until 1933 when it was demolished for a new suite for the
Connaught Rooms designed by Ashley and Newman, the architects
of the colossal new Freemasons' Hall next door.

Georgian terraces

**Above: 2–24 Bedford Row,
Holborn, 17 August 1908**
Much of Georgian and early Victorian London
owed its remarkable unity to the standardised
approach to elevations drawn up by estate
surveyors. The design of the houses and the
wider layout of an area were infused with a
classical proportional system based on the
Imperial system of measures. This can be seen
clearly here on the east side of Bedford Row. Note
the telegraph wires on the roofs and the valances
with retractable external Venetian blinds.

**Right: 1 Bedford Square, Bloomsbury,
1 July 1913**
Ground floor rear room. The plain exterior of the
London terrace house often concealed ornate,
enriched interiors.

Clubland

Right: 74 St James's Street, 22 April 1945
Designed by George Basevi and Sydney
Smirke in 1844 as the Conservative Club,
No. 74 is one of the most handsome
frontages in an area renowned for its
understated, urbane architecture – but here
it is looking tired and shabby at the end of
the Second World War. The Club closed
in 1959. Following restoration, it is now
occupied by HSBC.

Below: Clubland epitomised. View of the
Library with square columns and pedestals
of multi-coloured scagliola and gilt
mouldings. The leather chairs, mahogany
furniture, leather-topped tables and well-
stocked library all convey the quiet repose
of an exclusive gentlemen's club.

A merchant's palace

Above: Crosby Hall, Bishopsgate, 8 June 1907

One of the great private merchant's houses of mediaeval London, Crosby Hall was built between 1466 and 1475 for Sir John Crosby, whose tomb (1476) lies in the nearby Church of St Helen, Bishopsgate. In 1909 the great hall was dismantled and re-erected at Danvers Street, Chelsea Embankment, under the supervision of Walter Godfrey for the British Federation of University of Women. In 1993 the Chelsea site was sold and the hall reverted to its original purpose as part of a magnificent neo-Tudor private residence for a City trader. The mediaeval bay window is enriched with armorial stained glass. From 1868 the hall was used as banqueting rooms. The base of the bay window is a bar.

Above left: 20 Spital Square, c.1900
Grand five-bay houses of this type were erected for prosperous merchants, bankers, brewers and weavers. Built in 1732, the house was remodelled extensively around 1790 when the basement and ground floors were refronted. The arch-headed doorway with its leaded fanlight and Coade stone mask and dressings were fashionable later alterations. The guilloche frieze and wrought iron railings also date from this period. The house still survives.

Top centre: The superb entrance hall (c.1790) with its screen of Corinthian columns and delicate neo-classical plasterwork.

Above centre: 30 Spital Square, 6 November 1908
Ground floor room: this spectacular carved chimneypiece (c 1739) was one of four which were salvaged and sold when No. 30 and its neighbours were demolished in 1922.

Top right: 25 Spital Square, 22 April 1909
The remarkable entrance hall (1733) with alternating fluted and twisted balusters to the staircase. Masked consoles carry the cornice with richly-detailed rococo plasterwork above.

Above right: 22 Spital Square, 4 May 1909
Entrance hall and staircase (c.1733) with splayed steps, twisted balusters and raised and fielded panelling.

Old aristocratic mansions

Above: Cumberland House, Pall Mall, c.1907
In 1760 the Duke of York, the younger brother of George III, purchased a group of houses on the south side of Pall Mall, and commissioned Matthew Brettingham Snr to design a substantial new town house. On his death in 1767, it passed to the Duke of Cumberland who enlarged the courtyard and built the projecting wings, including the two gate lodges by Robert Adam. In 1806 it passed to the Boards of Ordnance, later the War Office, which occupied it until it was pulled down in stages for the Royal Automobile Club between 1906 and 1912.

Left: Buckingham House, Pall Mall, c.1906
John Soane's magnificent staircase compartment. The original colour scheme would have been striking – blue-grey walls, marbled columns with bronzed capitals and bases to the Ionic columns. In 1855 Buckingham House was acquired by the War Office, which continued to occupy it until 1906. Two years later it was demolished to make way for the Royal Automobile Club.

Lost at cards

Above: Harcourt House, Cavendish Square, 11 June 1906
Harcourt House, built by Lord Bingley in 1722–23 and designed by Thomas Archer, occupied the whole of the western side of Cavendish Square. Lost at cards by Lord Harcourt in 1825, it passed to the reclusive Duke of Portland who commissioned Thomas Cundy to rebuild the main frontage seen here. Regarded as "*a dull, heavy drowsy-looking house, which has about it an air of seclusion and privacy almost monastic*" (*Old and New London*), its seclusion was increased by high perimeter screen walls of cast iron and ground glass. The medallion over the entrance is of Inigo Jones. The white crosses mark items for salvage before demolition.

Below left: First floor ceiling. The delicate painted plasterwork suggests a house that was far from dull and heavy inside.

Below right: The staircase and entrance hall in the process of stripping out and demolition.

Great institutions

**Above: Royal Institution,
Albemarle Street, 8 April 1943**
The wealth from London's rapidly growing
global commerce funded some of its greatest
institutions. The Royal Institution was founded in
1799 for the advancement of science. In 1837–38
the windows were regularised, and a grand screen
of fluted Corinthian columns with capitals based
on the Temple of Mars Ultor was superimposed
over a group of earlier 18th-century houses by
Lewis Vulliamy. In this wartime view, the sign
outside the front entrance denotes a bomb shelter.

Left: Royal Institution, 29 March 1949
The elegant split staircase of c.1775 is probably by
John Carr of York with the double lyre pattern,
wrought-iron balustrade typical of his work. The
marble statue of Michael Faraday presides over
the entrance hall. Behind is a bronze cartouche
of James Dewar, the chemist and physicist. To
the left is a large, early-19th-century cylindrical
electro-static generator.

Aristocratic splendour

Above: Norfolk House, 31 St James's Square, c.1910
Norfolk House was one of London's great aristocratic
town houses with an understated, grand nine-bay
frontage designed by Matthew Brettingham between
1748 and 1752. This view shows the drawing room,
with its coffered ceilings and lavish gilded plasterwork,
designed for entertaining and to impress the visitor with
the wealth and power of England's premier dukedom.

Right: 22 Arlington Street, c.1910
One of London's finest interiors, 22 Arlington Street was
built in two phases between 1740 and 1750 by William
Kent for his patron Henry Pelham, who became Prime
Minister in 1743. The *tour de force* is this magnificent
Great Room with a fantastic coffered ceiling of red and
blue panels enriched with grisaille mythological figures.
In this view it is cluttered with pot plants, tables and
Edwardian furnishings. It has now been incorporated
into the adjacent Ritz Hotel.

Lost riverside masterpiece

Left: Adelphi Terrace, 6 March 1913

The Adelphi, developed by the Adam brothers between 1768 and 1774, involved building high over the Thames foreshore on a vast complex of subterranean arches to the level of the Strand. The scheme covered several streets to the south of the Strand, and was saved from bankruptcy by a parliamentary lottery.

Adelphi Terrace was the centrepiece, but its relationship to the river was transformed by the construction of the Victoria Embankment in 1864–70. Two years later the terrace was rendered and vulgarised and a central pediment added. The Adelphi was demolished amid great public outcry in 1936.

Below: The brick arches beneath the Adelphi were a Piranesian world of vaulted cobbled streets lit by shafts of light from portholes above. A small part of this atmospheric complex still survives off York Buildings beneath the later Adelphi development.

The Strand and bustling Piccadilly

Left: 73 Strand, 30 August 1908
In order to complete the Adelphi scheme, Adam Street was cut through to the Strand. No. 73 was completed to Robert Adam's design in the 1770s. After a disastrous fire in 1822, it was rebuilt to the same design. The elaborate ornamental ironwork to the Adelphi Wine and Spirit Stores was fashionable in the late 19th century. Beyond lies the massive Hotel Cecil.

Below: 107A Strand, 24 July 1908
The elegant frontage of John Burgess & Son with the royal warrant over the entrance.

Above: Piccadilly Circus, c.1895
The heart of the Empire and the vibrant hub
of London's louche nightlife. Albert Gilbert's
Shaftesbury Memorial – the Angel of Christian
Charity – actually depicts Anteros, the brother
of Eros, the god of requited love, who symbolises
the selfless philanthropic love of the Earl of
Shaftesbury for the poor. The awkward angled
geometry of the Circus has always generated
challenging traffic problems.

Right: Duchy House, The Strand, 1899
Duchy House occupies a corner site on both The
Strand and Wellington Street, since renamed
Lancaster Place. Dating from 1897, it is now
used as accommodation for students of the
Courtauld Institute of Art.

Westminster

**Above: 32 Abingdon Street,
20 August 1910**

32 Abingdon Street stood at the corner with Old
Palace Yard. Designed in 1723 in the style of William
Kent, it was an exceptionally handsome town house
in an austere Palladian style.

**Opposite below: Houses of Parliament,
c.1890**

A view of the Palace of Westminster, designed
by Charles Barry and built between 1837 and
1858. In the foreground Parliament Square is
filled with horse-drawn traffic.

Right: 10-11 Downing Street, c.1925

Downing Street was developed from 1682. To the right, the facade of No. 10 dates from 1766–74, subsuming an earlier house by William Kent of 1732–35. The two central bays of No. 10A were incorporated into the four bays of No. 11, to the left, in the 1770s. No. 12, the curious single storey 'stump' is all that remains of an earlier house of 1682, which was destroyed by fire in 1879. In 1960–63 the entire complex was remodelled and extended by Raymond Erth.

Grand plans

Admiralty Arch, The Mall, Westminster, 1913
The newly completed Admiralty Arch. Sir Aston Webb's remodelling of the Mall, Buckingham Palace and the completion of the Queen Victoria Memorial was one of the finest examples of grand axial planning in Europe, transforming the old ceremonial heart of London into a magnificent new Imperial capital.

Opposite above: Criterion Restaurant and Theatre, Piccadilly Circus, 26 October 1902
The Criterion was one of London's largest dining rooms, with a French Empire style frontage of 1871–74 by Thomas Verity. The arched central entrance led to the famous Long Bar, the setting for the meeting between Sherlock Holmes and Dr Watson in Conan Doyle's famous stories. The superb Byzantine interior of gilded mosaic and American marble was revealed under sheets of plasterboard after decades of neglect during its restoration in 1984. Spiers and Pond were railway caterers, and the Criterion marked their first foray into the West End.

Above: Criterion Restaurant, Piccadilly Circus, 1913
The first floor Great Hall of the Criterion at 2.50pm with paired Corinthian pilasters, painted friezes and curved coffered ceilings lit by a central dome. The tables are set for a formal dinner. A small dais has a piano for entertainment.

West End elegance

Below: Slaters, Kensington High Street, 1909
The jams and pickles counter at Slaters was typical of many shop interiors of the period, with elaborate Art Nouveau glazing, mirrored counters and elegant displays of produce.

A mediaeval fantasy

Left and below: Tower House, 29 Melbury Road, Kensington, c.1895

Built for his own use by William Burges between 1876 and 1878, Tower House boasts one of the most spectacular interiors in London, with superb structural decoration and painted stencilled details in the distinctive High Victorian style, which Burges perfected at Cardiff Castle and Castell Coch. The house remains in private ownership. In this view (top left) of the garden front, with Melbury Road beyond, there is little to suggest the mediaeval fantasy that lies within.

Each room had a particular theme. The Library, depicted below, was dedicated to the liberal arts with a full-blown Burgesian Gothic chimneypiece of The Tower of Babel with Nimrod and Queen Grammar sending out elements of speech. Adjacent is a superb cupboard painted with mediaeval scenes beneath an elaborate frieze and ceiling.

Burges's own bedroom (left) is a riotous fantasy of inventive Gothic iconography. It was decorated in deep red with convex ceiling mirrors to reflect candlelight. The mermaid chimneypiece is embellished in silver and gold with an unusual sinuous frieze of sea creatures. In the corner is a romantic mediaeval painted cabinet in the characteristic Burges style with his monogrammed initials at the base.

Albertopolis

Above: The Royal Albert Hall, Knightsbridge, c.1890
Opened in 1871 by Queen Victoria, the Royal Albert Hall was one of the key focal points in the development of Albertopolis, the cultural quarter laid out after the Great Exhibition in 1851. Measuring 20,000 square feet, at the time of its construction the roof was the largest dome without intermediate support in the world.

Right: The Natural History Museum, South Kensington, c.1900
A view of the museum from the Cromwell Road, showing its Romanesque facade. Designed by Alfred Waterhouse in grey and cream terracotta, it was opened in 1881, originally as an extension of the British Museum.

Old Admiralty House

**Left: Old Admiralty,
Whitehall, May 1935**
The famous Old Admiralty Board Room from which many of Britain's greatest naval victories were directed. The spectacular carved pearwood garlands, trophies and musical instruments over the fireplace are attributed to Grinling Gibbons; the coffered ceiling above of 1786–87 is by S P Cockerell. The focal point of the room is a wind compass controlled by a weathervane on the roof, and painted with a map of the British seas, coastal waters and allegorical figures.

Below: Old Admiralty House, 1935
The main entrance hall behind Thomas Ripley's portico of 1723–26 is plain and understated with Doric pilasters and swags above. In the niche is a statue of Nelson by E H Baily (1844), the near life-sized original model for Nelson's Column. Suspended from the ceiling with the royal crown is a late-18th-century lamp which belonged to the old Navy Board.

Top: St James's Palace, 25 July 1907
St James's Palace remains the official residence of the sovereign. Ambassadors are accredited to the Court of St James. Substantial areas of Henry VIII's palace remain, including the Gatehouse and Chapel Royal. The Throne Room is the spatial culmination of the State Rooms, which were reworked extensively by Nash in the 1820s with enriched coved plaster ceilings. Beyond the gilded throne canopy lie the doors to the Council Chamber.

Above left: Admiralty House, Whitehall, May 1935
Entrance hall and split staircase to Admiralty House designed by S P Cockerell. The panel in the centre of the staircase is inscribed with the names of the First Lords of the Admiralty.

Above right: Admiralty House, May 1935
The groin vaulted kitchen of Admiralty House complete with its range, dresser and kitchen utensils. Naval banquets were prepared here for the First Lord, who occupied the main house.

A school of manners

Opposite: Carlisle House, Carlisle Street, c.1910
Completed in 1687, Carlisle House was probably
built by three speculative builders on the
western edge of Soho Fields. From 1763 until
the early 1780s it was the residence of Domenico
Angelo, riding and fencing master to the Prince
of Wales, and the most fashionable school of
arms and manners in London. David Garrick,
Thomas Sheridan, George Stubbs and Sir Joshua
Reynolds were frequent visitors, after which it
was subdivided as it became less fashionable. It
was destroyed by enemy action on 11 May 1941.

Left: 75 Dean Street, 1 April 1912
The well-known painted staircase, falsely
attributed to Sir James Thornhill, or his son-in-
law, William Hogarth. The house was the subject
of an unsuccessful battle to secure parliamentary
confirmation of a Preservation Order under the
Ancient Monuments Act 1913. After a two-
day hearing in a select committee, the owners'
petition was upheld. The house was demolished
in 1923, but the staircase, hall and ground floor
rooms were re-erected in the Art Institute of
Chicago.

**Right: Little Wild
Street, 11 June 1906**
Interior of the Baptist
Chapel and Mission
Hall with a ventilating
gasolier suspended
from the ceiling.

POVERTY

When Charles Booth completed his monumental 17-volume work *The Life and Labour of the People in London*, it was the most comprehensive survey of the social condition of the capital ever carried out. Commissioned to disprove socialist claims that a quarter of Londoners lived in poverty, what it revealed was infinitely worse.

In the golden age of Edwardian England, one-third of all Londoners – about 1.8 million – lived below the poverty line. For a further one million, life was precariously balanced with just a week's wages between respectability and pauperism. Illness, bereavement or accident could condemn a family to instant destitution. The highest concentration of poverty – 68 per cent – could be found south of the river between Blackfriars and London Bridge followed by Greenwich with 65 per cent.

The worst social conditions – both moral as well as physical – were linked directly to the actual plan and grain of a district. Blind streets, yards and alleys approached via a single entrance tended to harbour the worst extremes of deprivation and crime. Some of these can be seen here – Dickensian warrens of sunless courts and alleys; houses cheek by jowl with toxic industries; melancholy streets caked in a penitential garb of soot, where the arrival of the photographer was a major event prompting whole families to stand outside their squalid houses in poignant group portraits. Poverty is etched indelibly into the faces of the people. The very houses carry the stamp of poverty; the brickwork around the doors rubbed smooth from countless arms and shoulders as people took whatever light and air they could. Theirs was a bleak, harsh world of unremitting grind. In 1905 the average age of death in the West End was 55. In the East End it was 30.

"No more dreary spectacle can be found on this earth than the whole of the awful East … the colour of life is grey and drab. Everything is helpless, hopeless, unrelieved and dirty", wrote Jack London in his haunting portrait of the *East End – People of the Abyss*. Over one million people from all corners of the earth were crammed into a vast labyrinth of insanitary streets, courts and alleys, where life was dominated by the daily search for work, food and shelter. It was a place of poverty, hardship, crime and degradation, but one leavened by an indomitable sense of humour and a deep-seated sense of community, a place where people pooled resources to share the basic necessities of life – such as a pair of boots or a simple bonnet.

Across London 300,000 people lived in one-room tenements. Over 900,000 were housed in illegal lodgings or doss houses. Weekly renting was the norm. 90 per cent of the poor had no home they could call their own beyond the end of the week. Often rooms were occupied on a relay system with two or three tenants each occupying the same vermin-ridden bed with the space beneath let on a similar basis. Living conditions for the poor were a shocking reproach to Edwardian England. By 1905 Dr Barnardo had saved over 60,000 destitute children from appalling squalor, vice and degradation, but thousands of the most vulnerable still slept on the streets.

Spitalfields, Stepney and Whitechapel were a huge ethnic melting pot where waves of immigrants settled in a desperate bid to build better lives. For many, London was a hard, unyielding place, but for those who made it, it offered independence, opportunity and freedom; not least freedom for political exiles and radicals to ferment international revolution. Ironically, Mazzini, Garibaldi, Marx and Engels, Litvinov, Kropotkin and Lenin and Stalin, all found sanctuary in the capital of the greatest empire the world has ever known.

But poverty was not just confined to Bankside, Borough and the East End. For centuries the north side of the Strand was characterised by a maze of mediaeval passages and courts. The first wave of bubonic plague began here in 1665. Clare Market and the area around Drury Lane was a notorious slum with a formidable reputation for crime. Living conditions in parts of Westminster were as bad as parts of the East End. Within 500 yards of the Palace of Westminster lay scenes of unimaginable squalor where streets of once-refined 17th- and 18th-century houses had descended in to use as cheap lodging houses. The ubiquitous pawnbroker provided a vital lifeline to many, offering short-term loans against items of value.

"London is a shameful tale of two cities. It is the richest capital of Europe, but half our children live below the poverty line. These families are cut off from the life most Londoners take for granted. They are the dispossessed". But this was not written by Charles Booth, Jack London or Charles Dickens. It was the conclusion of an in-depth study in 2010 by the *Evening Standard*.

Opposite: 9-11 Shepherd Market, 4 November 1911: Shepherd Market serviced the grander houses of Mayfair, but in 1911 it was an enclave of dingy, rundown streets surrounded by great wealth.

In the shadow
of Parliament

Above: Parliament Street, 1909
View from the east side of Whitehall looking
south towards Parliament Square. To the
extreme right is the corner of the Foreign Office
on what is now the junction with King Charles
Street.

Middle left: Scotts Rents, Smith Square, c.1910
These mean little 18th-century cottages stood
in a small yard in the south-east corner of
Smith Square, and originally were built as
cheap rented dwellings, probably for unskilled
workers. The dog to the left of the picture is
chained to the wall.

Bottom left: Grubb Street, 21 May 1906
Living conditions in parts of Westminster
were as bad as parts of the East End. Grubb
Street was characteristic of the grinding
poverty of the Millbank area, which was rebuilt
comprehensively from 1900–39.

**Right: Princes Street,
31 August 1909**
View looking south towards the
rear of the Westminster Hospital.
Beyond the porch is a cast-iron
street urinal. Of the two now
remaining in London, only one is
still in use.

Above: Princes Street, c.1909
Princes Street looking north to the
junction with Great George Street.
The handsome five-bay house with
the raised projecting, pedimented
porch is c.1720. The entrance to
Princes Mews can be seen just
beyond.

Right: Charlotte Street, c.1890
For generations immigrant communities have left their mark on London's neighbourhoods. The Germans settled in Fitzrovia, until internment during the First World War. It is a measure of their impact that the Queen's Arms at the junction of Tottenham Street and Charlotte Street was covered with advertisements for German beers and lager.

Below: The Dover Castle, Westminster Bridge Road, Lambeth c.1890
A dazzling interior of painted glass and ornate plasterwork with mahogany panelling and bar fittings. For the poor, the palatial interior of a London gin-palace was the grandest building many ever experienced.

Opposite: Ye Olde Kings Arms, Eltham, 1900
A fine 17th-century twin-gabled public house, which stood opposite the parish church until it was demolished to allow for road widening in the 1920s for a tram-route extension.

Above: 38–40 Tufton Street, 21 May 1906

A once-handsome pair of early-18th-century houses in use as lodging houses. The photographer appears to have attracted keen interest with faces at virtually every window.

Colonel Blood, who attempted to steal the Crown Jewels in 1671, is reputed to have retired to the previous house on the site with a royal pardon and a pension, fuelling suspicions that he had been acting on behalf of the King. The house was distinguished by a carved brick shield and coat of arms, but was demolished for the buildings seen here.

Cheap lodgings

Top: 66 Leman Street, Whitechapel, 8 February 1910
Manor House Working Man's Home: a once grand 18th-century merchant's house in use as a common lodging house for the working man. Rooms varied from 5d to 6d a night or 2/6d or 3/– per week. The house still survives. The "Surgeon-Accoucheur" to the left, marked by a distinctive red globe lantern, offered medical care and midwifery to those who could afford it.

Above: 62 Leman Street, 8 February 1910
The fine 18th-century panelled entrance hall and staircase fallen on hard times.

Ramshackle survivors of the Great Fire

Above: Nos. 13a–15 Nevill's Court, 16 March 1910
This remarkable group of 17th century, pre-Fire houses on the north side of the court had small courtyard gardens enclosed by wooden palings. Keir Hardie lived for several years at No. 14. Christabel Pankhurst was another notable resident.

Right: Nos. 13a–15 Nevill's Court, 16 March 1910
Oblique view of the front elevations of the buildings which were in use as lodging houses, before their demolition in 1912. The remainder of Nevill's Court was swept away in 1929 to create a new road from Shoe Lane to Chancery Lane.

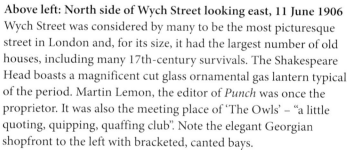

Above left: North side of Wych Street looking east, 11 June 1906
Wych Street was considered by many to be the most picturesque
street in London and, for its size, it had the largest number of old
houses, including many 17th-century survivals. The Shakespeare
Head boasts a magnificent cut glass ornamental gas lantern typical
of the period. Martin Lemon, the editor of *Punch* was once the
proprietor. It was also the meeting place of 'The Owls' – "a little
quoting, quipping, quaffing club". Note the elegant Georgian
shopfront to the left with bracketed, canted bays.

Above right: Drury Court, 11 June 1906
Drury Court linked Drury Lane with the Strand. The portico of
St Mary-le-Strand can be seen in the distance. To the left, is Ben
Jewell, a Rags, Bones and Fat merchant. The gap site next door
shows the truncated timbers and laths of a timber-framed house.

Between Wych Street and the Strand

Opposite below right: Windsor Court, 22 April 1901
Windsor Court was typical of the foetid courts and alleys of
mean dwellings which provided shelter to some of London's
most deprived people.

Above: Newcastle Street, 11 June 1906
The east side of Newcastle Street between Wych Street
and the Strand. The area was renowned for its dealers
in second-hand furniture, bedding and old clothes. The
Globe Theatre, which held 1500 people, had its pit and
stage underground, the dress circle and boxes being level
with Newcastle Street. Another entrance in Wych Street
provided access to the gallery and royal box.

Changing use

Opposite: The Earl Grey, Straightsmouth, 1913
A once-fine 18th-century merchant's house with an elegant timber doorcase in use as a public house. It was not uncommon for ordinary domestic buildings to be used as public houses.

Above: Vere Street, 11 June 1906
This early-18th-century corner building was formerly The Blackmoor public house, which gave its name to Blackmoor Street, a continuation of Clare Street. The plaque on the splayed corner depicts two negroes' heads, the initials S.W.M. and the date 1715.

Right: Blackmoor Street, 9 October 1902
Blackmoor Street was a narrow thoroughfare linking Drury Lane with Clare Street. A side entrance to Clare Court can be seen to the left. The beehive above the shop to the right was popular with wax chandlers, but also used as a trade sign by drapers and hosiers.

Rural vernacular

Top: **1, 3 & 5 Perrins Lane, Hampstead, 17 November 1908**
18th-century weatherboarded cottages with The William IV public house beyond. The site was redeveloped for modern mews houses in the 1960s.

Above: **Three Crowns Inn, 1–3 High Bridge, Greenwich, 1936**
With its twin bay windows and weatherboarded walls, The Three Crowns was typical of many riverside public houses that once lined the lower reaches of the Thames.

Top: **Pemmell's Court, Church Street, Greenwich, 23 November 1911**
View of an unusual range of very narrow, three-storey weatherboarded 18th-century houses hidden in a narrow alley between Nos. 13–15 Church Street.

Above: **2 St Paul's Lane, Rotherhithe, 1911**
This view demonstrates the remarkable extent to which timber-framed vernacular buildings survived in areas like Rotherhithe well into the 20th century. Pantiled roofs, stained weatherboarding and ramshackle backyards had more in common with the riverside villages of the Thames estuary than inner London.

Rotherhithe – an isolated riverside village

Above: 1–9 Purnell Place, 8 November 1911
Rotherhithe is effectively a peninsula sandwiched between the Thames and the former Surrey Docks. Rotherhithe Street is the long, sinuous thread which once drew together a host of riverside communities. Purnell Place was a short cul-de-sac, facing open ground, behind the former Stave Dock.

Above right: View of the rear elevations showing the massive chimney stacks, weatherboarding and mixture of pantile and tile roofs. The population of Rotherhithe trebled in the 19th century, and these small houses were home to the poorest classes who worked the waterfront and docks.

Right: 302–312 Rotherhithe Street, 8 November 1911
A wonderful view of the backs of the houses seen above, which were built as a terrace with weatherboarded, gabled outshots and huge chimney stacks. Beyond is the looming mass of a mid-19th-century warehouse at Globe Stairs.

A warren of sunless courts

Bankside: views taken on 16 May 1912
In 1902 Charles Booth revealed that the highest concentration of poverty in London – 68 per cent – could be found in the area between Blackfriars and London Bridge. Poisoned by toxic fumes from nearby white lead, gas and engineering works, the squalid maze of dingy streets and sunless alleys behind Bankside contained some of the worst housing in London. All the following images were taken on 16 May 1912.

Left: White Hind Alley
"The surrounding streets are mean and close; poverty and debauchery lie festering in the crowded alleys …; an air of gloom and dreariness seems … to hang about the scene, and to impart to it a squalid and sickly hue." (Charles Dickens, *Pickwick Papers*).
   White Hind Alley was a narrow passage lined on one side by mean dwellings and on the other by a high wall to a timber yard which blocked out the light to the houses.

Below left: Moss's Alley
Parts of Moss's Alley were less than 8ft wide, but provided access to a whole nest of small subsidiary courts and yards crammed with families categorised by Booth in the lowest class as semi-criminal, along with occasional labourers and loafers, their children classified as street "arabs".

Above: Wagstaff Buildings, Bankside
Wagstaff Buildings was a narrow back alley of dark weatherboarded and brick dwellings sandwiched between an engineering works, which can be seen to the left centre of the picture, and Great Guildford Street.

Opposite right: Cork's Place
Cork's Place (formerly Pleasant Row), which connected with the southern end of Wagstaff Buildings, was lined with industrial works and an iron foundry. To the right is the rear of properties in Zoar Street – another dreary street of two-storey early-19th-century dwellings.

Right: Bermondsey Square, 9 October 1900
Loan offices and pawnbrokers were common in poor neighbourhoods such as Bermondsey but they provided the only safety net for those out of work or facing destitution.

CHANGE

London was the first great metropolis of the modern age. In 1800 it was a major European capital of one million people. By 1911 it was the largest city in the world – greater than the combined populations of Paris, Berlin, St Petersburg and Moscow. This phenomenal expansion was unique, creating a city unlike any other with its own distinctive form and character.

As London expanded outwards from its twin centres in the City of London and Westminster, whole districts were laid out to a common pattern by surveyors using the Imperial system of measures and proportion. Everything deployed in the construction of public spaces, houses and their internal furnishings derived from the human form, which accounts for the remarkable unity and visual cohesion of Georgian and Victorian London.

One of the unique features of this city was, and remains, the London square. Terraces of individual houses, each subordinated to the wider composition, were laid out around communal gardens enclosed by railings for the pleasure of surrounding residents. By 1900 there were over 460 across the capital. As well as providing oases of green space, they created a highly distinctive urban grain which imparted a unity to the city and connected the wealthiest with the poorest neighbourhoods.

Much of the subsequent development of London led to the fragmentation of this unified whole – with the advent of the railways, road widening, metropolitan improvements and the construction of much larger buildings on aggregated plots for a whole variety of new uses. Nevertheless, a great deal of this urban backcloth still remains, in areas such as Islington, Bloomsbury, Hackney, Camberwell and Lambeth.

With the development of public transport, London embraced, and later subsumed, outlying villages, as low-density suburbs spread across the Home Counties. As a result, many of London's urban villages retain much older cores.

The distinctive character of the Victorian city was castigated by many as remorselessly monotonous. Dickens lamented its unremitting shabbiness. By 1900 London was

Opposite: Euston Station, c1895: Planned by Robert Stephenson for the London end of his London to Birmingham Railway, Euston Station opened in 1837; the first mainline terminus in a capital city anywhere in the world, its entrance triumphantly heralded by the colossal Euston Arch designed by Philip Hardwick. Despite a protracted campaign to preserve the Arch during reconstruction of the station, its demolition in 1961 and the subsequent outcry was a landmark in the development of the modern conservation movement in Britain.

an extraordinary kaleidoscope of districts with a constantly shifting social geography as areas declined, prospered or were redeveloped with bewildering rapidity – a process which continues to this day. Older domestic buildings and areas were swept away as large swathes of London were transformed into a great commercial and Imperial capital.

In Whitehall, the government precinct was transformed as the great offices of state in old 17th- and 18th-century houses gave way to a magnificent new generation of government palaces. The very heart of ceremonial London was remodelled to reflect the Imperial zeitgeist. In 1912 Sir Aston Webb completed its reconfiguration with a spectacular example of monumental axial planning from Trafalgar Square through the new Admiralty Arch to a new rond-point at the Victoria Memorial and on to Hyde Park Corner. The entire east front of Buckingham Palace was refaced in just three months, replacing Edward Blore's lacklustre façade.

The momentum of civic improvement continued relentlessly. The Holborn to Strand improvement scheme, which had been under discussion for over 60 years, was the largest single clearance of buildings since the Great Fire, overseen by the newly founded London County Council which specified height limitations and a classical style. Beneath Kingsway a modern tram tunnel was constructed, entered from beneath Waterloo Bridge and emerging at Theobalds Road.

Further west the reconstruction of Nash's Regent Street began simultaneously. The gradual accretion of signs, fascias, awnings, royal warrants and blown coats of paint over the original bare Roman cement finishes so impaired the original composition that many welcomed redevelopment. The authorities simply specified fire-resisting construction, Portland stone, a uniform height of 60ft to the cornice, and two roof storeys at a 75 degree pitch in green Westmoreland slate, but completion took almost 30 years.

In the City and West End large areas were rebuilt in Edwardian Beaux Arts style – an expression of civic pride and Imperial self-confidence. In the City new citadels were raised for banking, shipping and insurance. Across the capital palatial new buildings arose which expressed the political and commercial might of the British Empire.

By 1939 the population of London was 8.2 million – well ahead of New York with 6.93 million – the seat of the monarchy, the government and the judiciary. It was widely acknowledged to be the finest city in the world, but it was also a shockingly vulnerable target on the brink of catastrophe and massive unimaginable change during the Second World War.

Working river

Top: Lett's Wharf, c.1912

In the mid19th century desperate bands of women sifted rubbish here for anything which could be recycled. Later it became a refuse depot and part of the industrial South Bank. Today it is the site of the National Theatre. In the distance to the right of the chimney is the tower and spire of St John's, Waterloo.

Above: Tower Bridge, c.1889

Construction began in 1887 to designs by Sir Horace Jones, the Architect and Surveyor to the City of London, and Tower Bridge opened in 1894. It was designed as a bascule bridge, so that the central section could be raised to allow the passage of ships to and from the busy wharves of the Pool of London.

Above: Horse Shoe Brewery, 268–268 Tottenham Court Road, 1906
Looking east across Tottenham Court Road towards the Horse Shoe
Brewery, the premises of Meux's Brewery Company at the corner of
Tottenham Court Road and Oxford Street. The brewery was demolished
in the 1920s to make way for the Dominion Theatre.

Sadly demolished

Top: 1–13 Euston Square, c.1937
Euston Station formed the centrepiece of an elegant square of stucco terraces built in 1811 as an extension of Bloomsbury to the south. This terrace stood on the north side at the east end. Only the wreathed lamp column, part of the war memorial, remains.

Above: Columbia Market, Bethnal Green, 1870
The brainchild of the philanthropist, Baroness Burdett-

Coutts, Columbia Market, in full Flemish Gothic style, opened in 1869 but closed just 16 years later, before being used as workshops by the London County Council. Sadly, this splendid landmark building was demolished in 1958.

Opposite: Walsingham House Hotel, Piccadilly, 1899
Walsingham House Hotel, here seen from Piccadilly, stood on the site now occupied by the Ritz Hotel. It was built in 1887 and demolished in 1904 to make way for the Ritz.

Above: Orange Street Congregational Chapel, St Martin's Street, 23 July 1906

The Chapel was used by the Huguenots from its foundation in 1693 until 1787, when it was taken over and converted into a Congregational chapel, which closed in 1917. A small replacement chapel was built in 1929 in Orange Street. The adjacent house was the home of Sir Isaac Newton from 1711 until his death in 1727. Fifty years later Fanny Burney lived there. Dr Johnson, David Garrick and Sir Joshua Reynolds were frequent visitors. The house and chapel were demolished in 1913 for Westminster Public Library.

Left: Exeter Hall, Strand, 1907

Exeter Hall was the centre of the anti-slavery campaign and a bastion of radicalism. Many famous speeches and meetings were made within its walls. Livingstone, Stanley, Brougham, Shaftesbury, Clarkson and Wilberforce all "took the chair" at Exeter Hall. In 1880 it was taken over by the YMCA, after which it was remodelled and enlarged. It was demolished in 1907 to make way for the Strand Palace Hotel. The organ was sold and relocated to Ipswich Public Hall.

Children's refuge

The Foundling Hospital, Guilford Street, Holborn, c.1912

Above: The Foundling Hospital was established in 1742 by Captain Thomas Coram. In the early days, abandoned babies were left here for the hospital to take in as foundlings, but due to the sheer level of demand a ballot system was introduced. The splendid chapel was renowned for its organ which Handel gave to the hospital and on which he played several performances of Messiah raising over £7,000 in funds. The chapel became fashionable, attracting many eminent figures, including Dickens who lived nearby in Doughty Street. The font, pulpit and organ were relocated to the chapel of the new hospital at Berkhamsted in 1926.

Right: The austere, vaulted Boys' Dining Room with bench seating.

Top: Chesterfield House, South Audley Street, May 1932
With a spectacular French rococo interior, Chesterfield House was regarded as one of the finest aristocratic town houses in London. In 1922 it became the home of the Princess Royal before it was sold and demolished in 1937.

Left and opposite above: Dorchester House, Park Lane, c.1927
The spectacular central staircase and marble chimneypiece. The house was pulled down in 1929 to make way for the jazzy new Dorchester Hotel designed by Curtis Green.

Lost mansions of Mayfair

Above: Chesterfield House, South Audley Street, May 1932
The splendid marble staircase and screen was designed
by James Gibbs in 1715 for Canons, the great house of the
Duke of Chandos at Stanmore, which was demolished in
1748. When Chesterfield House was pulled down in 1937,
the staircase was salvaged once again for use in a cinema in
Broadstairs where tragically it was destroyed in the war.

Top right: Devonshire House, Piccadilly, 1920
In 1897 the Piccadilly frontage of the house was embellished
with a beautiful set of wrought iron gates and piers from
Chiswick House. With the demolition of Devonshire House in
1924 they were moved once again – this time to the entrance
to the tree-lined avenue in Green Park leading from Piccadilly
to the Victoria Memorial.

Opposite below right: Devonshire House, Piccadilly, 1920
The exquisite ceiling of the Saloon.

**Above: Gamage's Department Store
and the Prudential Building, Holborn, 1907**
Crowds outside A W Gamage's department store in Holborn
on sale day. A W Gamage started a small shop in 1878, and it
became one of London's leading department stores before its
final closure in 1972. Beyond is the Gothic Revival Prudential
Building, designed by Alfred Waterhouse in phases from 1879.

Right: General Post Office North, St Martin's le Grand, 1903
Designed by Sir Robert Smirke and opened in 1829, the General
Post Office was one of the most elegant buildings in London
with a grand Greek Revival frontage. A new GPO building was
opened on the site of Christ's Hospital in King Edward Street
immediately to the west in the same year – 1911– that Smirke's
landmark was demolished.

Opposite: Globe Theatre, Newcastle Street, 1902
Posters advertise "Sweet Nell of Old Drury" at the Globe
Theatre. The theatre opened in 1868 and closed in 1902; it
was subsequently demolished for the Holborn-Kingsway
improvement scheme.

Modernising transport

Opposite above left: Leicester Square Underground Station, Cranbourn Street, 1916
An interchange for the Piccadilly and Northern Lines (then the Hampstead Line). The corner houses the premises of Salmon & Gluckstein, tobacconists.

Opposite above right: Hampstead Underground Station, 1907
Hampstead Tube Station, the deepest on the network, advertised as 'now open' after the Northern Line, on which it lies, was opened by David Lloyd George in June 1907. One of Leslie Green's characteristic designs in dark maroon faience, the station has separate entrances and exits to avoid congestion during the commuter rush-hour.

Opposite below: Fenchurch Street Station, 1912
Designed by George Berkeley in 1854, Fenchurch Street Station was originally the terminus of the London and Blackwall Railway. The destinations served by the station are set into a frieze under the canopy. A horse-drawn carriage advertising "summer excursions" is parked in the forecourt.

Above: Junction of Wych Street and Holywell Street, c.1910
The Rising Sun was a fine Elizabethan tavern. The frontage facing St Clement Danes boasts a brash new illuminated sign for "Dewars Whisky" obscuring the old Elizabethan structure behind, but the gabled roof and railed parapet of its neighbour bear witness to its early origins. The suspended lantern is a veritable leviathan.

London landmarks

Above: St George's Hospital, Hyde Park Corner, c.1910
A view of St George's Hospital taken from the first floor of Apsley House, popularly known as No. 1 London. Built between 1827–33 in neo-Greek style to the designs of William Wilkins, the great central portico is based on the Choragic monument of Thrasyllus. The hospital closed in 1980. After standing vacant as one of London's most prominent buildings at risk for about 10 years, in 1991 it was converted into the exclusive Lanesborough Hotel.

Opposite above: St Thomas's Hospital, 1878
Originally founded by monks in the 12th century, St Thomas' Hospital eventually relocated south of Westminster Bridge in1871 on land reclaimed during the construction of the Albert Embankment. The pavilions were designed by Henry Currey as Nightingale wards to maximize light and ventilation to the wards and to reduce the risk of cross-infection.

Opposite below: Dorchester House, Park Lane, 1905
Completed in 1857 to the designs of Lewis Vulliamy and modelled on the Palazzo della Farnesina in Rome, the house was one of the most opulent private residences in London. After use as a hospital during the Great War, it was demolished in 1929 to make way for the Dorchester Hotel.

Pantheon – Oxford Street

Left: The Pantheon, Oxford Street, 1937
The original Pantheon, designed by James Wyatt, opened in 1772 for concerts and masquerades. Gutted by fire, it was reconstructed as a place of assembly, and in 1811–12 converted to a theatre, which was short-lived owing to restrictions imposed by the Lord Chamberlain. In 1833-34 it was rebuilt as a bazaar by Sydney Smirke, who retained and adapted Wyatt's altered frontage, replacing the portico with his own design carried on cast-iron Doric columns.

Above: The great barrel-vaulted hall, on the first floor, which was used by W and A Gilbey, the wine merchants, as a showroom and offices from 1867. In 1937 the Georgian Group tried to negotiate the re-erection of the facade, as part of a new country house at Chilgrove, Sussex, but it came to nothing. The building was demolished shortly after for a new Marks & Spencer store in sleek, black moderne style by Robert Lutyens.

Regent Street

Right: 170–160 Regent Street, 1913
Robinson & Cleaver's department store in the throes of demolition. This striking block was designed by Sir John Soane and completed in 1821 in his characteristic style with simple incised pilasters. The much-altered central pavilion is crowned by a figure of Mercury flanked by eagles. To the north, a run of ladders is fixed to a huge flagpole.

Above: 144-122 Regent Street, 1913
Sainsbury's is at No. 136. The flank elevation at the extreme right shows the change in height and scale of the new development which progressively replaced Nash's original buildings.

Left: 98 Portland Place, Regent's Park, 10 September 1946
View of the north-east corner of Portland Place at the junction with Park Crescent. By 1946 many of the grand Regent's Park terraces were in a shocking state of disrepair as a result of poor original construction and bomb damage. Following a government committee, the Crown Estate embarked on a phased programme of sensitive repair, refurbishment and development. Park Crescent was reconstructed behind the retained original facades between 1960 and 1963.

Destruction

Above: King Square, Finsbury, 2 February 1945
Idealistic post-war planning destroyed more
of London's historic neighbourhoods than the
Luftwaffe. King Square survived the war, but
tragically the buildings were cleared for uninspiring
public housing by Finsbury Borough Council in
the 1960s.

Right: St Barnabas, King Square, January 1941
Designed by Thomas Hardwick in 1822–26,
St Barnabas was the focal point of King Square,
its thin needle spire, a local landmark. Although
the surrounding buildings were swept away, the
church was restored and reopened in 1956.

**Opposite: 22–40 Great Cumberland Place,
Marylebone, 1941**
View of the east side showing the damage caused
by enemy action. Surface street shelters can be seen
on the semi-circular forecourt. Subsequently the
terrace was restored.

Abandonment

Above: Swedenborg Square, Stepney, 19 August 1945
View of the west side of Swedenborg Square with a street shelter to the right. The pilasters have been removed from the doorcases, prior to demolition.

Left: 21–26 Houghton Street, 11 June 1906
View looking south to the junction with Newcastle Street showing demolition in progress. The shop on the extreme left offers "Cupids Whispers" and "Select Old Charms Tobacco" in the window alongside "Selected Fine Fresh Eggs".

Above: 22–26 Wellclose Square, Stepney, 30 July 1943

Today it is difficult to comprehend the shabbiness of wartime London or the sheer scale of destruction. Many streets of once-fine Georgian houses were abandoned and boarded up after bomb damage.

   View of the west side of Wellclose Square showing a surviving mid-18th-century timber house with a fashionable Serlian window to the ground floor. Adjacent is a later 18th-century derelict terrace with a wartime street shelter marked with white stripes for visibility in the blackout.

FREEHOLD
FOR SALE
or to be
LET on BUILDING LEASE
All applications to be made to SOLE Agents
HAMPTON & SONS
2 & 3, COCKSPUR ST,
Pall Mall.

On the eve of demolition

Opposite: 15 & 16 Buckingham Street, c1905
These late-17th-century houses at the south end
of Buckingham Street stood beside the old York
Water Gate. Used as the Prize Office from 1704–10,
and later by the Institute of Civil Engineers, No. 15
was the residence of the architect William Burges
between 1875 and 1881. When it was pulled down
in 1906, two ceilings and various fixtures were
relocated to the new building on the site. No. 16
has a fine shallow bow window and carved masks
to the window arches.

Right: Salisbury Street, c.1890
Salisbury Street was rebuilt as a single architectural
composition in 1783 by the architect James Paine,
flaring out into a shallow curve at the southern end.
Too narrow and too steep ever to be fashionable,
it was sold in 1888 and pulled down shortly after
for the Hotel Cecil, which in turn was replaced by
Shellmex House in 1930.

Below: Cumberland Market, Somers Town, c.1930
View of the south side west of Osnaburgh Street.
Cumberland Market was a market for hay brought
in from the country via the Regent's Canal. The
large setted space in the foreground shows its
original purpose. The entire area was redeveloped
for public housing in the 1930s.

Left: Madame Louise, 266–268 Regent Street, 1912
View across a quiet Oxford Circus towards the south-east corner and the milliner's shop Madame Louise which boasts the latest Paris fashions.

Below: Marble Arch, Hyde Park, c.1900
Marble Arch, designed by John Nash in 1827 as the ceremonial gateway to the refurbished Buckingham Palace, was moved to its present position at the corner of Hyde Park in 1851. In 1908 a new road, Cumberland Gate, was cut across the corner of the Park leaving Marble Arch stranded on a traffic island.

Tranquil quarters

Above: Tower of London, c.1900
A view east from Tower Hill with Tower Bridge
visible to the right. The Tower was built in
the 11th century on the orders of William the
Conqueror and extended by future kings. The
White Tower, in the centre, is flanked by outer
towers. From left to right: Bowyer Tower, Flint
Tower, Devereux Tower, Beauchamp Tower and
Bell Tower.

Right: Thames Embankment c.1890
Horse-drawn vehicles travel along the Thames
Embankment on the north side of the river.
Cleopatra's Needle and Waterloo Bridge can
be seen in the distance, with Somerset House
beyond and the river frontage of the Savoy Hotel
to the left.

Left: Nelson Square, Southwark, 1940

View of the north side of Nelson Square (built between 1804–18) showing taped up windows to mitigate the effects of bomb blast. Beside the first floor windows of the house on the left are outdoor bird cages, once a common sight in inner London. Much of Nelson Square survived the war, but later was replaced with dull post-war council flats by Southwark Council. Only a fragment of the original terraces (Nos. 44–47) survives.

More books from Philip Davies and Historic England's archives

If you've enjoyed reading this publication you may be interested in the books shown below. *Lost London: 1870–1945, Panoramas of Lost London, London: Hidden Interiors* and *Lost England: 1870–1930*. These books are written by the best-selling author Philip Davies who has been at the forefront of managing change to London's most important buildings and places for 40 years.

Philip Davies is also the author of *Lost Warriors: Seagrim and Pagani of Burma – the last great untold story of World War II*.

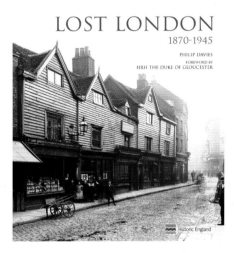

Lost London 1870–1945
Nearly 600 historic photographs show the capital's vanished past. '360 pages of sustained shock and awe...in pinsharp clarity' *The Times*
ISBN: 978-1-909242-95-1   368pp   £50.00

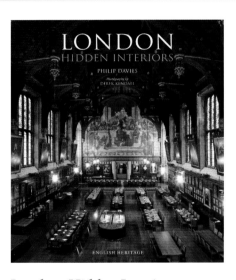

London: Hidden Interiors
1700 sumptuous photographs reveal in detail 180 of London's finest and most historic conserved interiors.
ISBN: 978-0-9568642-4-6   448pp   £50.00

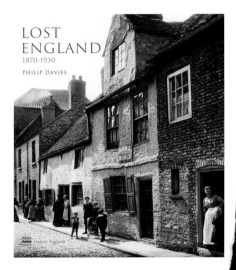

Lost England 1870–1930
The lost world of Victorian and Edwardian England is beautifully, and evocatively, discovered in 1,200 photographs.
ISBN: 978-1-909242-79-1   570pp   £50.00

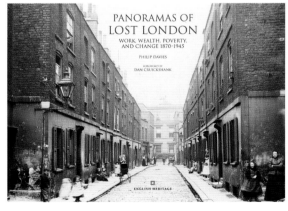

Panoramas of Lost London
Over 300 of the best images of Lost London enlarged into a landscape view.
'A glorious and monumental piece of work' Bill Bryson
ISBN: 978-1-907176-72-2   320pp   £50.00

Lost Warriors: Seagrim and Pagani of Burma
The gripping tale of two very different men thrown together by chance in the depths of the Burmese jungle. Hugh Seagrim, the complex soldier and Christian mystic in search of the meaning of life, and the pugnacious Roy Pagani, who risks death repeatedly in his bids for freedom.

A true story of honour, courage, love and self-sacrifice in the face of appalling brutality.

'beautifully written, extraordinarily interesting; moved me to tears' John Simpson BBC
ISBN: 978-1-909242-85-2   272pp   £20.00